The
MINDSET
LIST
OF THE
OBSCURE

74 Famously Forgotten Icons from

A *to* Z

TOM McBRIDE A

Coauthors of the Beloit ... ot List

 sourcebooks

Published by Sourcebooks, Inc.
P.O. Box 4410, Naperville, Illinois 60567-4410
(630) 961-3900
Fax: (630) 961-2168
www.sourcebooks.com

Library of Congress Cataloging-in-Publication Data
McBride, Tom, 1945–
  The Mindset list of the obscure : 74 famously forgotten icons from A to Z / Tom
McBride and Ron Nief ; coauthors of the Beloit College Mindset List.
    pages cm
  Includes bibliographical references and index.
  (trade : alk. paper) 1. Popular culture—United States—History—20th century. 2.
Nostalgia—United States—History—20th century. 3. Memory—Social aspects—
United States—History—20th century. 4. United States—Civilization—1970– I.
Nief, Ron, 1943– II. Title.
  E169.12.M2363 2014
  306.0973--dc23

2014021421

Printed and bound in the United States of America.
VP 10 9 8 7 6 5 4 3 2 1

TO THE PIONEERING FIGURES AND IDEAS THAT SHAPED
DAILY LIFE IN MID-TWENTIETH-CENTURY AMERICA

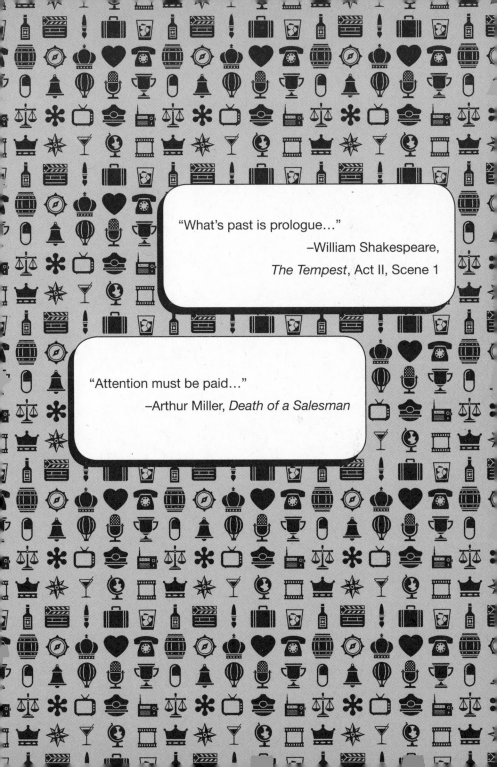

"What's past is prologue…"
—William Shakespeare,
The Tempest, Act II, Scene 1

"Attention must be paid…"
—Arthur Miller, *Death of a Salesman*

CONTENTS

INTRODUCTION

Few things are more pathetic, or at times funnier than encountering someone who is considered "out of date." When Mr. Burns on the television show *The Simpsons* wanted his nuclear power company to win a softball tournament, he asked his flunky, Smithers, to find him top players, such as Cap Anson and Pie Traynor. Unfortunately, Anson and Traynor were dead—and had been so for many years. Mr. Burns was so out of touch that the once-great players he insisted on were not only gone into the ground, but also almost no one remembered them anymore.

This book is about using the past to understand the present, through the lenses of cultural phenomena that are barely remembered today. Here is a feast of history and nostalgia, a cornucopia of comparative popular culture, by which we can learn about our own time by discovering—or being reminded of—what was so terribly popular or ignominious or appealing or repulsive so long ago. The list we have compiled ranges from once-indispensable technology to legendary performers and forgotten professions to the notorious, sensational language and expressions of yesteryear. What made these phenomena so successful or well known? Why are they forgotten now? How would they fare in the present time? This book illustrates why, if you want to understand the way we live *now*, you should look back at the way people lived *then*. We focus particularly on the experiences of those who are part of the Greatest Generation (World War II), but most commonly the Silent Generation (born in the 1930s and early 1940s) and the famous Baby Boomers (born after World War II through the early 1960s). The book shows the truth of what William Faulkner once said: "The past is never dead; it's not even past."

The origins of this book go back to our work as the cocreators of the annual Mindset List, an international ritual every August in which Americans (as well as others around the world) take a look at entering college students: their assumptions, attitudes, their sense of what has "always" or "never" been considered normal in their short lives. Here are some examples:

- *"God has never been a 'he' in most churches." (Mindset List Class of 2005)*
- *"A coffee has always taken longer to make than a milkshake." (Class of 2010)*

A glimpse at each new generation's mindset is tinged with irony, of course, because what they might think has always been true has not been. As trackers of new trends, we have become, in the words of the *Seattle Times*, "America's cultural timekeepers," a duty we do not take lightly. We have become avid students of the generation gap, not just in its present form, but all across the panorama of American history. And we have become convinced of what this book exemplifies: that if you know how to do it, a look at the past illuminates the culture of the present.

As cocreators of the annual Mindset List, we are constantly attending to the question of how things have changed. Today, singing telegrams are to smartphone apps as the horse and buggy was to the automobile. In the 1950s, a fictional rich man gave away a million dollars each week on TV. That would be worth nearly nine million dollars today. Most Americans alive today were born after President Kennedy was assassinated and have no real idea of what that national trauma was truly about. On a lighter note, few Americans today remember when Bob Barker invoked Beulah the Buzzer as a sentence to undergo embarrassing practical jokes on a television game show. Such contrasts are useful barometers of both present and past. They measure monetary inflation, track what different generations mean by "the Kennedy Tragedy" (for those under forty, the plane crash of JFK Jr. off Cape Cod may be much more vivid than the murder of his father in Dallas), identify the vital differences between digital and nondigital messages, and even make us think about whether TV game shows are any less fatuous now than they were back then. Beulah the Buzzer is gone, but one current game show cohost has become world famous for doing nothing but turn a wheel of fortune. What has changed, and what hasn't really changed at all? Only by studied comparison of past and present can we approach this question with the care it deserves.

This book is meant to be both a record of the past and a light shone upon the present. It is meant for readers of many ages. As is often the case when we visit the past, we are amazed at what people once thought was funny, disgusting, exciting, or technologically advanced. If you are a grandparent or parent, give this book to your descendants. You and they can share a good laugh at the expense of the past, and they can learn a lot about what the world was all about when you were young. How else will they learn how many animals Flub-a-Dub was made of or how poetic Percy Dovetonsils was or what rabbit ears or slide rules were? There are some things that our "young and restless" simply must not get to age forty without knowing! This book might also gently remind them that someday, someone will write a book casting a baleful eye on what *they* once thought great or appalling. The critical eye of the young gets us all in the end. Someday, even Katy Perry and smartphone apps will seem hopelessly out of date. Meanwhile, as Arthur Miller once said of his hapless salesman Willy Loman, "attention must be paid" to what has become obscure, if only as a cautionary tale about the hot current stuff that is likely to become obscure in the future.

We could go on and on. In fact, we *have* gone on and on—and it's all in this book. We hope this amusing and informative (and maybe even a little provocative) book is more than a trip down memory lane. It's also a way to spark insight into our current time, with its milieu of always rapid and sometimes bewildering trendiness. You may not agree with all our assessments of what these past phenomena say about the present, but we trust that you will be stimulated to think about the question.

This book is organized from A to Z, from "A&P" to the "Zapruder film." Any cross-references in the book are **bold-faced**. Each item includes:

- *a brief timeline to provide context for its cultural heyday*
- *an inspired guess by "Today's Young and Restless": what today's young people, if asked, might guess an item refers to or means*
- *a brief essay that reveals each item's once-famous identity and meaning and the circumstances of its fading away*

- *an assessment of how the same phenomenon would fare in the present day*
- *a hypothetical usage of the item in a sentence as uttered by those who lived during the time when everyone knew what the item meant. These speakers are the "Old and Settled"—a counterpoint to the "Young and Restless."*

This book concludes with a piece called "Here's Your Change," a brief overview of this volume's contents that answers the question of whether everything has indeed changed over the past half century or more. Was Shakespeare right when he suggested the past is prologue to the future—and even to the present? The nature of change and the linkage between past and present and future are enduring mysteries. We hope this book will clarify them.

Tom McBride
Ron Nief

A&P

WAL-MART BEFORE WAL-MART

TIMELINE: A&P was founded in 1859; by 1900, there were two hundred stores. By 1930, there were sixteen thousand.

INSPIRED GUESS BY TODAY'S YOUNG AND RESTLESS: Two of the three letters needed to spell "app."

THE ANCIENT TRUTH: A&P is the name of a grocery store chain, a corporation once as famous as McDonald's or Target and just as dominant in the American consumer market. It was, as the *Wall Street Journal* once said, "Wal-Mart before Wal-Mart." It was founded in the nineteenth century in New York City and was first known for its teas and coffee; eventually, as it expanded into sugar, baking soda, and lots of other products (mostly foodstuffs), it termed itself "the Great Atlantic and Pacific Tea Company." A&P stores stood out among other grocery stores in their design features.

Some stores actually had faux crystal chandeliers to help you find the green beans (fresh or canned but not yet frozen), and you could buy your forty-five-cent can of one pound Eight O'Clock coffee from a checkout lady in a seersucker dress sitting in a checkout stand shaped to resemble a pagoda.

In the 1930s, a tenth of Americans bought their groceries at an A&P store.

Hardly ever undersold, A&P offered sharp price reductions based on business of gargantuan volume and pioneered the use of cheap, generic "house" brands, such as Eight O'Clock coffee and Jane Parker cakes. A&P was mammoth; its "integrated" tentacles found their way into not only the stores that sold food, but also the warehouses that stored it and the trucks that carried it. Long before the monster food chains did so in the late twentieth century, A&P drove many independently owned "Mom and Pop stores" out of business. Mom and Pop were politically powerless—but the big food distributors were not. Knowing that Mom and Pop would have to pay them higher prices than A&P would, the big distributors went to Congress and called A&P a monopoly. But A&P countered that Congress shouldn't want Americans to pay higher prices for butter and green beans, and with that argument, A&P won the political battle.

But then came something that even A&P could not fight: prosperity.

Post–World War II America was richer. It demanded bigger, cleaner stores with national brands, like those advertised on TV with the basso ho-ho-ho of the Jolly Green Giant and the wise-guy fish

Charlie for StarKist Tuna. For Depression-era America, A&P with its cheap house brands was a boon; for Eisenhower's more affluent America, the cost cutting of A&P was no longer required. A&P tried to respond with larger and more noticeable stores, featuring such architectural notables as cupolas and weather vanes. It was too late. Soon a German corporation (the Tengelmann Group) bought the great but now-struggling Atlantic and Pacific icon. To this day, there are still A&P stores in various parts of the United States, particularly on the East Coast. Compared to the chain's grandeur of yesteryear, these stores are few and far between.

For anyone who laments the younger generation's unfamiliarity with the phrase "A&P," there is an indelible sliver of hope: college students are often assigned a 1961 story by John Updike called "A&P." Professors ask their students to read the story because it's a riveting tale of what happens when rich snobs invade the puritanical middle-class realm of the local A&P store. Updike traces the clash of classes and culture with exquisite precision and drama.

THAT WAS THEN, THIS IS NOW: For Americans during the first half of the twentieth century, "normal" shopping tended to involve going to several different stores for various items; there was no such thing as a "one-stop shop." Coffee was purchased at the grocery store, but you had to go to the hardware store for light bulbs. And for them, it was normal to ask the clerk to retrieve what they requested, which was often time-consuming. For today's generation, "normal" is a superstore, part of a much, much larger chain, where a huge variety of products is for sale and where they, not a clerk, select them. For years now, self-service has been as normal as a pair of black socks, and with the Internet, it's even possible to cut out the human checkout clerk. But we should remember the A&P in its heyday as one of the great precursors to today's "big boxes." Though small by comparison with today's Walmarts, they were among the very biggest boxes around.

HYPOTHETICAL USAGE IN A SENTENCE BY THE OLD AND SETTLED:

"Do you want me to stop by the A&P to see if they still have kidney beans, six cans for a dollar?" —Uncle Arthur speaking to Aunt Bea, around April 29, 1946

ABBOTT AND COSTELLO

WHO'S ON FIRST?

TIMELINE: Abbott and Costello first worked together in the mid-1930s in New York City. They got on the radio in 1938, which was also the premier date of their most famous skit "Who's on First?" Their popularity continued through the '40s and '50s.

INSPIRED GUESS BY TODAY'S YOUNG AND RESTLESS: Abbott must have been that guy Elvis Costello's first musical partner.

THE ANCIENT TRUTH: Bud Abbott and Lou Costello were the number-one comedy duo in the United States in the 1940s. Into the early 1950s, they were in both radio and film's top ten. They were enormously popular, perennially famous, and extremely profitable—only rivaled later in that period by Dean Martin and Jerry Lewis. They started off as New Jersey vaudevillians—performers on the live variety

show stage that marked American life during the Gilded Age—and Costello added to his own résumé, for a while, the title of amateur boxer. Vaudeville was eventually displaced by movies and radio, but it was also the gift that kept on giving, as nearly all the great performers in the new media of radio and film came out of vaudeville, where they found their talent, honed their acts, and sharpened their timing. This was especially true for comedians. Abbott and Costello were poster kids for this genre of vaudevillians who made it big in radio and film.

They were best known for a single radio routine called "Who's on First," a spoof that started with the premise that baseball players were developing weird nicknames (such as Dizzy and Daffy Dean of the St. Louis Cardinals). Thus why not have a player named *Who* on first base, a *What* on second, and an *I Don't Know* on third? The mayhem and confusion of such a premise produced a frenzied hilarity, and Abbott and Costello could do the banter speedier than a one-hundred-mile-per-hour fastball.

The angular Abbott was always the straight man, and chubby Costello played the bumbling dunce with the near-soprano voice. The more earnest Abbott put up with Costello, not because he thought a little humor made life whole, but because the laughs made the dough—piles of it. Although they made nearly forty films together and had an addictively popular radio show, bad health, alcoholism, family tragedy (the accidental drowning of Lou's baby son), and even a near split ravaged their partnership—for a whole year, the two only spoke to each other when performing. They did a little early television, but Lou died young and Bud was never good as a solo act. They probably would have fared poorly on television. The media guru Marshall McLuhan always said that TV was a "cool" medium; intense people didn't go over well on it because they were too "hot" for viewers' living rooms. This might well have been true for Abbott and Costello: too hopped-up for the tube.

Today's generation knows nothing of Abbott and Costello, but they may have picked up a reference or two. The '90s television show *Buffy the Vampire Slayer* once mentioned the boys, and Montclair State University in New Jersey has a residential wing named after them. Today's young might also have seen a sequel to "Who's on First" performed by Jimmy Fallon, Billy Crystal, and Jerry Seinfeld—available on YouTube since 2012. The revival of a classic is always welcome news to those who hope for its ongoing endurance. In early 2014, the skit had enjoyed nearly one million hits.

THAT WAS THEN, THIS IS NOW: For listeners and fans at the time, the madcap zaniness of Abbott and Costello won rave reviews, and "Who's on First" depended on baseball, which was (and remains) the nation's beloved national pastime. For today's generation, a more laid-back, cool, and cynical form of comedy has become the norm, and baseball's "American" quality has suffered by the greed of its owners and the chicanery of its drug-assisted players. Even so, let's remember "A&C" as one of the best examples of how the greatest American comedy of the mid-twentieth century was born of now-forgotten vaudeville.

HYPOTHETICAL USAGE IN A SENTENCE BY THE OLD AND SETTLED: "I'm so confused about this math problem that I'll go further than Abbott and Costello: to me, 'I Don't Know' is on *every* base." —Anonymous, around 1950

#3 AIMEE SEMPLE McPHERSON

LADY IN THE PULPIT

TIMELINE: The height of Aimee's fame was between the 1920s and early '30s.

INSPIRED GUESS BY TODAY'S YOUNG AND RESTLESS: A famous sharpshooter of the Old West.

THE ANCIENT TRUTH: Aimee Semple McPherson was the most famous female Christian evangelist in American history. In the 1920s, and indeed up until her death in 1944, she was a household name and as well-known as Oprah is today. McPherson didn't live all that long—her successful but much less celebrated son, also in the religion business, survived ninety-three years compared to her mere fifty-four. But she at least died famous.

McPherson was born Aimee Kennedy on a farm in Salford, Ontario. It's hard to describe someone as "religiously precocious," but if anyone was, it was she. As a girl, she led her playmates in games of "Salvation Army." She was also an inquisitive high school student who was deeply disturbed by Darwin's theory of evolution. She quickly caught on to the fact that Darwin's theory was inconsistent with the Bible's literal account of creation. Her teachers could not tell her how to make science and religion coexist in peace; she decided she must choose one or the other. In fact, McPherson hated the theory of evolution all her life, because she thought it not only a lie, but also a product of satanic logic.

On this pious note, in 1908, she married a missionary named Robert Semple, with whom she went to China, where they both contracted malaria. Although she survived, her husband did not. After she got out of China in 1910, she settled in New York with her almost equally pietistic mother, Minnie, working for her beloved Salvation Army. Soon enough, Aimee, ostensibly dying in a 1914 New York hospital, heard a voice that said: "Preach!" And so she recovered and did. It wasn't only a question of a divine calling, but also one of technical excellence, for both Aimee and Minnie realized the former had a creative gift for public presentation. She, her second husband Harold McPherson, and her mother went on the road and sojourned amid some economic hardship to send the Gospel's good news. By the late teens, Aimee had become one of the most charismatic preachers in the United States and Canada. She attracted thousands to a revival service by carrying a large banner around a boxing arena during a prizefight. It read "Knock Out the Devil." She practiced speaking in tongues. Blessed with a beatific laugh and an erotic demeanor braced by wholesomeness, she preached vivid sermons, often laced with portentous allegory rooted in modern life and embossed by spectacular playlets. And in time, her long itinerant travel on behalf of the Lord led her to Los Angeles, where, in the 1920s, she reached her greatest success. By this time, L.A. was growing fivefold, from one hundred thousand to over five hundred thousand in just a decade. McPherson grew with it. In 1927, she founded her own Pentecostal sect, called the Foursquare Gospel (not to be confused with the current smartphone app Foursquare)—and built an awesome mosque-like temple to go with it. She took on a denominational identity: "Sister" Aimee. There were enough seats in Aimee's temple for over five thousand souls, plus standing room for a few hundred more. It was the first "mega-church." There were services every day of the week, several times a day.

> Sister Aimee bought a mansion on a lake in the Golden State, proving that while the meek may inherit the earth, those who speak for the meek on loudspeakers get the fine view. In the late summer of 1925, McPherson was away from Los Angeles and wanted to fly there in time for Sunday service. With two thousand devotees waiting to meet her at the airport, the plane crashed. She boarded another forthwith. That plane made it. She arrived in time to preach and said that day that the first plane was piloted by the Devil and the second by Jesus Christ.

Aimee never would have become nationally famous without the radio. She was only the second woman in history to get a radio license. She was soon heard in L.A. and then throughout the country. By 1925, she had gotten caught up in the conflicts then roiling American social life. On one side were those who wanted to play cards, dance, attend the theater, and embrace science but still have something in the way of a spiritual life. On the other side, to which McPherson belonged, were the more traditional forces and values. For McPherson and many others, religion could never be just incidental. Her Foursquare Gospel was built on four great doctrines: salvation, baptism, healing, and Christ's return.

Despite her traditionalist beliefs, McPherson was in fact a rather modern person herself. She advocated contemporary inventions, such as the airplane and radio. Above all, she supported women's rights, particularly to vote. She was a good example of a career woman and demonstrated that she could evangelize just as well as her male counterparts.

And then came the infamous incident for which she will always be most remembered.

In 1926, McPherson purportedly drowned on a California beach. Mother Minnie preached that night's sermon and reported to hosannas of woe that Aimee would not be coming back. One man even drowned trying to find her. But then Aimee showed up about two weeks later in the desert between Arizona and Mexico. She said two varmints named "Steve" and "Mexicali Rose" had kidnapped her with plans to sell her into white slavery. She'd gotten away and then walked hours through the vast desert (this has obvious biblical overtones) until she was found. Speculation was that she had fled to have an abortion or plastic surgery or that it was all about publicity. Further inquiry suggested that she had more likely run away with her radio producer and holed up in a hotel with him. Police investigated and a grand jury was convened, but there wasn't enough evidence for a conviction. Aimee stuck to her story until the end.

The country was divided over this garish episode, but women tended to side with Aimee. She was one of them. After that, though, her career went into a tailspin. She and her mother fought over control of the denomination, by now spread out in "lighthouses" all over the land. The Great Depression made her spiritual entertainments a bit beside the point. Now it wasn't Satan but hunger that the country had to worry about. She had a nervous breakdown. The city of Los Angeles that had once welcomed her now thought her embarrassing; it seems that L.A. was in the grip of a modernist malady. In 1944, she died of an apparent accidental overdose of a sleeping sedative.

THAT WAS THEN, THIS IS NOW: What would contemporary young people think of Aimee Semple McPherson? They would find her an anachronism, for according to a report on National Public Radio, many of today's young people use religion as a form of meditation rather than a ticket to heaven. They find the disapproval of gays by conservative American churches to be both intolerant and intolerable. And they find many of the old stories that Aimee liked, such as Abraham's being willing to sacrifice his own son because God told him to, an incredible farce. At a time when people of all ages seem to be struggling with their faith and spirituality—trying to find a space for belief between science and religion—McPherson's zeal and cult following would seem hopelessly old-fashioned. Still, she ought to be remembered today for a simple but powerful reason: whatever her traditional values might have been, she was, despite herself, a progressive figure. She showed that a woman can be a great evangelist, which paved the way for others like her.

HYPOTHETICAL USAGE IN A SENTENCE BY THE OLD AND SETTLED:
"Where have you been? I bet you were 'kidnapped' by the same folks who tried to snatch Aimee Semple McPherson—or so she said."
—Mrs. Keenan speaking to Mr. Keenan, who habitually stayed out late, in about 1930

ARTHUR GODFREY

FIRED
IN FRONT OF
MILLIONS

TIMELINE: Arthur Godfrey reached his heyday in the late 1940s and '50s as one of the superstars of early television.

INSPIRED GUESS BY TODAY'S YOUNG AND RESTLESS: A character in an overlong Victorian novel.

THE ANCIENT TRUTH: Arthur Godfrey's father *was* English (and Victorian too), but Godfrey himself was the biggest name in television in the 1950s, on the air five days and two nights a week. Even the smash hit comedian Milton "Mr. Television" Berle never saw that much airtime. It had never happened before, and it has never happened since. It would be unimaginable today, at a time of incessant trendiness when media "overexposure" is always a risk.

Back then, there was no Internet, and there were only three major television networks (NBC, CBS, and ABC), so consumers had fewer entertainment options. Still, how likely is it that Arthur Godfrey, who had no dazzling talent of any sort, would have high ratings on a morning talk show, a weeknight amateur talent show (which once rejected Elvis Presley), *and* a weeknight variety show? A half century later, few remember Godfrey, and those few are dwindling by the day.

Godfrey came up the radio ranks in Washington, DC, and got his biggest break when, describing the funeral of Franklin Roosevelt in 1945 for a national radio audience, he gushed, "God bless you, Harry Truman," and broke up in tears. It was a spontaneous and candid outburst that electrified the country. Godfrey had dared share with the national public his own overwrought state, which matched theirs. He was one of them. Finally, he made the transition from radio to television in a manner that made him a much bigger TV than radio star.

While in his twenties, Godfrey became a navy radio operator—a crack one—and from that stint got into commercial radio at a time when it was becoming a dominant medium. Although he was badly injured in an auto accident on his way to flying lessons in 1931, he remained an avid aviator and supporter of commercial air travel. In the 1950s, he would often reassure his television fans that flying all the way to Hawaii for a holiday was quite safe.

What was Godfrey's appeal? He could chat. He was the master of palaver. Observing that most radio announcers were stiff and formal baritones, he concluded there was a market for soft-speaking, neighborly, spontaneous, folksy tenors. On TV, he appeared for several hours every morning with his soon-to-be-famous features: commercial sponsors such as Chesterfield cigarettes, Singer sewing machines, Lipton tea, and Paper Mate pens; a personable basso announcer named Tony Marvin; singers such as Frank Parker and Julius La Rosa; and above all, Godfrey's constant stream of unpredictable chatter. He made fun of his new sponsors. When Paper Mate pens claimed their ballpoints could write through butter, Godfrey apologized on air for not having any butter around to ruin the ink. He displayed a Singer sewing machine, and when he could not figure out what one drawer was for, he insisted that it must be the place you hid a little bottle of scotch.

Such uncanny gabbing made Godfrey seem to millions the folksy, over-the-fence "character" that every neighborhood in America had: the town's "wit," the club's "clown." The avuncular redhead seemed to be familiar and reassuring, and he quickly achieved an iconic celebrity status. But in time, as the 1950s trod along, it seems that the fame may have gone to his head. He emerged as a nasty control freak, a rigid man who liked humiliating his "little Godfreys" (the singers and announcers who were regulars on his morning show). And then one day, he fired one of his most appealing singers, Julius La Rosa, *on the air*. He announced "Julie's swan song." La Rosa had no idea this termination was about to come. It seems that Godfrey had become jealous of Julie's popularity. In light of the cruel dismissal, the nation recoiled against their once-beloved Godfrey, and his popularity quickly declined.

By the 1960s, he was no longer a prominent TV star but continued to broadcast on the radio. In his dotage, Godfrey was rather advanced in his thinking—an old codger who thought a bit like a maverick. He refused to allow Axion detergent as a sponsor when he discovered it contained phosphates that debased the natural environment, and he critiqued supersonic transport as an instrument of unbearable noise pollution. As a way to recapture some of his lost popularity, a joint TV appearance with Godfrey and La Rosa was scheduled toward the very end of his life, but the two men soon plunged into fussing again. The reunion was canceled. Godfrey died in 1983.

THAT WAS THEN, THIS IS NOW: An Arthur Godfrey could never happen today. He was on TV twelve hours each week (including at night in prime time) and on multiple shows for over a generation. Such exposure and longevity in a single personality would be almost impossible in today's rapid shift in fads and trends and the increasingly short attention span of TV audiences. Even the cordially ubiquitous Ryan Seacrest doesn't luxuriate in quite that much exposure. Godfrey thrived in an America with a lower threshold of excitement. *Time* magazine said he was the man with the "barefoot voice": it was a simpler time when sticking one's toes in the creek and just "chewing the fat" was exciting enough.

HYPOTHETICAL USAGE IN A SENTENCE BY THE OLD AND SETTLED: "This is your swan song, Julie." —Mr. Moore, speaking to his teenage daughter, telling her that this would be her last party after she came home two hours late (about 1956)

ARTHUR MURRAY

FIRST TANGO IN AMERICA

TIMELINE: The height of Arthur Murray's popularity was from the 1920s through the '50s.

INSPIRED GUESS BY TODAY'S YOUNG AND RESTLESS: Sounds like the founder of a root beer brand, or maybe an English fish and chips chain.

THE ANCIENT TRUTH: Arthur Murray (born Moses Teichmann in Austria-Hungary in 1895) was the founder of a once-thriving chain of dance studios. By the mid-1960s, there were over 3,500 locations. In his days of fame and glory, Arthur Murray—he changed his name in view of anti-German sentiment during World War I—was as synonymous with ballroom dancing as Fred Astaire was with tap dancing. In fact, in one film, when Astaire is asked who taught him to dance like that, he replies, "Arthur Murray."

Murray himself was shy and found that dancing

was a great way to overcome timidity and meet people. In his neighborhood in New York City, he would attend weddings just to practice his dance steps. A draftsman and reporter by day, he taught dancing at night. A gangly man who seemed preternaturally introverted and even robotic, he was the quintessence of graceful motion on the dance floor. He traveled around a lot—from Boston to North Carolina—and by 1920, he had organized the world's first "radio dance" atop an Atlanta hotel. He and his wife Kathryn began a flourishing mail-order business in which cutout footprints were sent to customers eager to learn the box waltz and tango. You placed the footprints on the floor in the prescribed sequence and stepped on them in the ordained order. Eventually you didn't need them, as the dance moves became second nature. Many people found this method to be an easy and accessible way to learn how to dance. He also authored books on the subject.

Arthur's great insight was that dancing was just a fancy form of walking. He believed that if you knew the steps, you could do the dance. And he understood that dancing was a swell way to get to know someone—because it is a publicly approved form of intimacy, and before people can share their deeper emotions, they must find a neutral subject, such as a particular dance, in common. Murray knew that friendly dance competition could be fun. Married couples bored with their lives could be transformed by the quest to win the silver cup against the Joneses or Smiths. And dancing was an easy way to impress the boss and his lovely wife and ensure that raise.

Arthur and Kathryn did not go gently into oblivion. Their 1950s TV show *The Arthur Murray Party*, which was a long testimonial to his dance studios, was one of only a handful to be featured on all four national networks (the fourth was the now-defunct DuMont). The program featured famous guests in formal evening wear, and at the end of the program, the tuxedoed Arthur and his gowned wife Kathryn would dance a great Strauss waltz. But the show's popularity eventually declined, and in 1956, the dancing scene changed forever with the appearance of another star known for his dance moves—Elvis Presley.

In the mid-1920s, Murray found a great new angle for his business: teaching dance across the country, first via instructors hired by the Arthur Murray Studios in the Statler Hotels across the land. In time, the studios became independent. Even some smaller cities, of around 30,000 potential steppers, had one. As late as the 1970s, you could see these abandoned buildings, with the unlit Arthur Murray neon sign still hanging.

THAT WAS THEN, THIS IS NOW: Did rock 'n' roll ruin the Murrays' dance party? There are a few hundred Arthur Murray International Dance Centers left, and according to their website, they are "the largest chain of dance studios in the world today." The popularity of ABC's *Dancing with the Stars* suggests that Americans are still interested in formal dancing, but programs such as Fox's *So You Think You Can Dance* and MTV's *America's Best Dance Crew* also hint at an appreciation for improvised, instinctive dance too. And if you want to learn how to dance the rumba or the box waltz, you can just watch YouTube videos. Still, Arthur Murray deserves to be remembered as the icon of a far more formal time in American life, when ballroom dancing was more than just fun; it was also a way to get ahead in American life.

HYPOTHETICAL USAGE IN A SENTENCE BY THE OLD AND SETTLED:

"Maybe Arthur Murray can save our marriage; Lord knows the counselor can't." —Your great-aunt speaking to your great-uncle, a month before serving him divorce papers, in 1946

AS AMERICAN AS APPLE PIE

PATRIOTISM ON A PLATE

TIMELINE: The heyday of this phrase occurred from about 1890 to about 1970. Sometimes the phrase is coupled with "motherhood" and becomes "as American as motherhood and apple pie," both once-hardy expressions of singular American values.

INSPIRED GUESS BY TODAY'S YOUNG AND RESTLESS: Probably the title of one of those old black-and-white movies they show on TCM.

THE ANCIENT TRUTH: It's not clear how apple pie came to be associated with all things good and wholesome about America to the point where the phrase "as American as apple pie" was once the leading simile of American speech. The expression essentially means "typically American." Yet the early colonists were more likely to eat meat pies ("pasties") than fruit pies, and the early usage of apples resulted in cider more often than pie. So usage alone cannot account for the popularity of the phrase. But there are other explanations. Perhaps one is that the taste of apples is distinctly American: sweet but tart, as though the greatness of the United States is that its people reward themselves after hard work but leave just enough sourness to remind them that they have to do it all over again tomorrow. Another explanation is alliteration: *America* and *apple* trip lovingly off the taste buds. Finally, there is the economic theory that during Prohibition, when apple cider was banned because it could be fermented, the apple industry kept its sales alive by claiming its product was distinctly American.

Whatever the reason, during the not-so-long-ago twentieth century, nearly everyone knew this expression, calling to mind Norman Rockwell scenes of Mom in the kitchen, spotless apron proudly worn, putting the freshly baked apple pie on the windowsill to cool. This would have been just an hour or so before the entire family sat down at the picnic table to celebrate the Fourth of July with streamers, bunting, fireworks (no sparklers allowed during supper), and hot dogs. Anything else would have seemed un-American, perhaps even anarchistic and certainly "immigrant." In those days, most Americans did not consider making guacamole on the Fourth.

But they thought of apple pie a lot, and not just on holidays. They even had an expression about apples keeping the doctor away, and sugared apples nestled in baked pie dough would do that job just as well. Only un-American sissies spent too much time down at the clinic. There was, after all, a country to be run.

THAT WAS THEN, THIS IS NOW: The phrase "as American as apple pie" assumed a uniform pride and patriotism. Even the Great Depression could not dent such strong national sentiment. But by

If you ask a young person today to finish the expression "as American as…," they might reply with anything from "couscous" to "Bart Simpson" to "rap." Or maybe they'd just reply "Apple," as in Steve Jobs. Will Apple someday perfect a virtual apple pie so that you can taste and smell the thing via digital magic? Will there be an iPie someday?

the 1970s, the old patriotism, in the wake of Vietnam and Watergate, began to wane. There were doubts about American purpose and morality. Apple pie continued to be beloved, but "as American as apple pie" had to compete with more lamentable comparisons, such as "as American as the Vietnam War Memorial" and with such books as *Real Men Don't Eat Quiche*, a 1982 satire on nonconformist masculinity as revealed by shifting, less "manly " culinary preferences. And today? Well, in a society fast evolving into a multiethnic rainbow, Americans can be found eating anything from chiles rellenos to soul food! But the expression "as American as apple pie" deserves to be remembered as a symbol of all things wholesome and good.

HYPOTHETICAL USAGE IN A SENTENCE BY THE OLD AND SETTLED:

"Honey, you're as American as apple pie—and that's why we're vacationing in Colorado, not Mexico, this year." —Your great-aunt speaking to your great-uncle after he reluctantly agreed that a vacation in Cancun was unaffordable—and unpatriotic—in 1950

BAKELITE

BEFORE THERE WAS PLASTIC

TIMELINE: Bakelite was invented in 1909; the Bakelite Corporation was founded in 1922. Bakelite was largely supplanted by lighter and more flexible plastics by the 1950s.

INSPIRED GUESS BY TODAY'S YOUNG AND RESTLESS: A magazine or blog of diet recipes.

THE ANCIENT TRUTH: Bakelite was the world's first great industrial plastic, at a time when the terms "Bakelite" and "plastic" were almost synonymous. A Belgian-born chemist, Leo Baekeland, invented the stuff in New York City early in the twentieth century. By the late 1920s, a factory in New Jersey was putting out mammoth amounts of it, and there were also associated companies and plants in England. In the late 1930s, Union Carbide bought the Bakelite Corporation. At its zenith, Bakelite was called "the material with a thousand uses." And Americans did use it: in telephone housing, radio housing, light bulb sockets, vacuum tubes, insulation of all sorts, brake pads, fountain pen housing, camera housing, machine-gun housing, and mah-jongg tiles (when the Chinese game was a fad in the United States). During a copper shortage, there was even talk of making pennies out of Bakelite. Heat shields for rockets and satellites employ an improved version of Bakelite today. If Bakelite had a thousand uses, even after all these examples, we are still 998 uses short.

Bakelite is a combination of phenol (a carbolic acid still used in Campho-Phenique, a first-aid potion sometimes used to treat cold sores) and formaldehyde, a chemical known for its rotten egg smell that can produce tears, fatigue, and headaches after prolonged exposure. In fact, if one rubbed a Bakelite product hard enough, a hint of this smell would appear. But there are no known instances of anyone getting high on Bakelite, because people wanted to use it, not sniff it.

Despite the famous advice given in 1967 to *The Graduate*'s young Benjamin Braddock by one of his father's friends—to go into "plastics" as a career—today we think little about plastics. But once, it was a phenomenal product, a twentieth-century miracle of convenience conferred upon the millions lucky enough to dwell in advanced countries. Bakelite and other plastics improved daily living through the magic of chemistry. With Bakelite, Dr. Baekeland took a building block of chemistry—molecules or atoms bonded together in a certain way—to create a synthetic moldable material that did not conduct electricity but did resist heat.

This, however, is not to say that Bakelite was perfect. It was heavy and drab, not equal to the light, multicolored plastic of today. By the time the featherlight but durable plastic of today, along with its garish colors, came along in the 1960s, plastic had ceased to be a miracle. Ironically, it was the monochromatic Bakelite that got all the *oohs* and *ahhs*, back when plastic of any sort was highly notable. Now plastic is about as remarkable to us as a microwave is. In fact, the microwave is probably housed in plastic.

Yet we should not take plastics for granted. Imagine the world we would live in if everything had to be housed in wood or metal. Think of how colorless the world would be, how heavy its artifacts. Bakelite was the pioneer of a most useful and lovely product. But by the 1950s, Bakelite started to become passé in the United States. It held on for another decade in England, whose relative poverty after World War II held its commercial technology back, but lasted longest behind the Iron Curtain, in the satellite countries of the Soviet Union such as low-growth Bulgaria and Albania. These countries were poor and accustomed to the heavy and drab. They enjoyed—or put up with—Bakelite well into the 1970s.

THAT WAS THEN, THIS IS NOW: Bakelite was a wondrous material when it first appeared in the period just after World War I. But in time, manufacturers and consumers alike wanted a more lightweight, versatile, and colorful plastic. Bakelite thus has become to today's plastics what the old Victrola has become to today's CD players—and even CD players are fast becoming obsolete! Yet there are still Bakelite collectibles, especially in jewelry. Watch for it on the television program *Antiques Roadshow*—emphasis on the word "antiques." Meanwhile, Bakelite deserves to be remembered as an homage to a slower, heavier, and perhaps more dignified time.

HYPOTHETICAL USAGE IN A SENTENCE BY THE OLD AND SETTLED:

"Put the salad in the Bakelite dish and let's go." —Winston Allyson, Saddle River, New Jersey, asking his wife to please hurry up, as they are late to a potluck supper with the neighbors, in about 1924

#8

BATHTUB GIN

NOT FOR BATHING

TIMELINE: It had its heyday from 1920 to 1933, but after the repeal of the Eighteenth Amendment and the end of Prohibition, there was no need to make gin in the tub.

INSPIRED GUESS BY TODAY'S YOUNG AND RESTLESS: A college party repository, next to the toilet scotch.

THE ANCIENT TRUTH: Bathtub gin was an illegal form of alcohol popular in the United States from 1920 to 1933, during the years when all liquor, wine, and beer were outlawed in the country. Thus "bathtub gin" took its place among a pantheon of illegal alcohols, with such names as "hooch," "white lightning," and, of course, "moonshine." The gin was not fermented in the bathtub, but the bottles required for the process were too tall for a sink faucet—so the bathtub faucet was used instead. The great forbidding that made this illegal but perhaps necessary was known as Prohibition, which was later called, after it failed, a "noble experiment." Today, historians see Prohibition as a cautionary tale of what happens when the government tries to deny an entire population a relatively harmless habit, one deeply rooted in their all-too-human propensity to relax and have fun.

Americans liked boozing. But they rarely smirked in public with open defiance of a law to ban it; instead, they promised to obey the law and then figured out myriad ways of breaking it. Among these—and among the most famous—was the manufacture of bathtub gin.

Grain is a wonderful thing—the very wheat and chaff of life— and a process known as distillation can glean alcohol from it. Distilled alcohol is the result of a rather rudimentary process of steeping grain alcohol with juniper berries and water in a large bottle. In the 1920s, however, grain alcohol was not always available, thus requiring the denatured alcohol that could lead to illness, blindness, or even death to unfortunate but desperate imbibers. Once it is distilled, alcohol can be fermented, and once that is done, it can make you drunk if you drink it. Getting drunk was generally the point. Americans knew that fermenting alcohol for purposes of inebriation was against the law. Small-time distillers knew there was a demand for it, however—especially by law-abiding citizens who went to Sunday school but dreamed of much racier pleasures—so they made the stuff, buttressed with juniper berries (seed pods known for their spicy taste, a flavoring technique that originated in the Middle Ages), and called it gin.

The full process was fairly simple. You simply mixed alcohol (preferably grain alcohol rather than the more dangerous denatured version) and water in equal parts. Then you placed the mixture within the large bottle. Steep the water and alcohol mélange with the aforementioned juniper berries, then store in a cool, dark place for two days, stopping by twice to shake the mixture with some vigor. Then pass the mixture through a strainer and, if you dare, drink, for you have gin! (That said, readers, don't try this at home! Keep the bathtub for rubber ducks only.)

Few ever said that stuff like bathtub gin was the best quality—in fact, it was infamous for its awful taste and possible toxicity—but thanks to the federal government, you had to take what you could find. It is difficult to estimate the rate of alcohol poisoning during this period because the government did not acknowledge the legality of alcohol and thus did not keep records. Nonetheless, according to a 2010 article by Deborah Blum, approximately ten thousand deaths may have occurred between 1920 and 1933 due to alcohol poisoning.

The distillers sold the finished product to Mafia gangsters (but also friends and neighbors) and then, having collected a tidy sum, started on the next batch. Behind the big pickup guys were even bigger guys with names like Al Capone. They dressed with garish aplomb, often had bulges at the tops of their suit coats, and brought about the cessation of those who got in their path. After all, booze were illegal, so mobsters couldn't very well go to the government to enforce their contracts. Breaches of agreements they handled on their own. Behind the bizarre bathtub gin enterprise was a lot of routine violence, even murder.

THAT WAS THEN, THIS IS NOW: Although bathtub gin has no place in contemporary American life—there is no motive to manufacture it—it's not just a relic of the 1920s. On the TV show *The Simpsons*, none other than Homer Simpson made the stuff and sold it to Moe's Tavern in Springfield. Other pop culture references exist: for instance, the rock band Phish had a 1999 hit song called "Bathtub Gin." Let us remember bathtub gin as a lesson about government overreach in the regulation of ordinary sin. Meanwhile, corn or dry whiskey— traditionally "moonshine" (once illegal)—is making a comeback. It is against federal law to make alcoholic beverages at home, but with the right permits from the Alcohol and Tobacco Tax and Trade Bureau, you can operate as a distilled spirits plant either for personal or commercial use.

HYPOTHETICAL USAGE IN A SENTENCE BY THE OLD AND SETTLED:

"Did you get this gin from the bathtub or the toilet?" —Aunt Mabel, around 1939, after Prohibition was over, wondering about the cheap gin Uncle John bought at what he claimed to be the corner liquor store

#9 THE BEARDED LADY

A STAR ATTRACTION

TIMELINE: The bearded lady was a popular carnival sideshow (or "freak show") figure in the mid-nineteenth century. These shows had declined in popularity by the early twentieth century.

INSPIRED GUESS BY TODAY'S YOUNG AND RESTLESS: A Border collie before she's been groomed.

THE ANCIENT TRUTH: The bearded lady was a top attraction in the popular circus sideshows or carnivals of the late nineteenth and early twentieth centuries. Bearded ladies sometimes had considerable facial hair, generally as a result of an imbalance of the hormone androgen. Associated with the bearded lady was a variety of sideshow characters, including:

- *the human torso (no limbs)*
- *conjoined (or Siamese) twins*
- *human skeletons (abnormally thin)*

- *the giant (abnormally large)*
- *the tattooed lady (self-explanatory)*

These unusual people were considered phenomena, and since traveling carnivals and circuses generally came through town only once a year, their exaggerated "freakishness" often drew enormous crowds and attention.

> Other sideshow attractions included the geek (not a computer expert, but one who bites off the heads of live chickens), the fire eater, and the sword swallower. Lunatic savages were presented as "the wild men of Borneo." Other sideshow attractions included Hitler's staff car (so claimed after World War II) and seminude women doing the "hoochie coochie." Four-headed goats and two-headed pigs were not excluded.

Today's baby boomers did not attend these sideshows as children, but they grew up hearing about them from their grandparents. Circus sideshows were part of the American lore that early boomers inherited, for by the early 1950s, the circus was just starting to fade as one of America's most popular live attractions. Sideshows were entertainment for a pre-radio and pre-movie society that had—at least by today's standards—an amazingly low excitement threshold. Today, in a world of constant sensationalism, we are not shocked by much. We don't need sideshow freaks that come to our towns once a year; we can get a similar thrill through the tabloids in our grocery store checkout lines, where we can read not only about the latest celebrity scandal, but also, in some of the more daring, about human chimps. We are likely to sigh at most, even if we give in once or twice a year and buy the *Enquirer* and hope the checkout clerk doesn't know us. Nineteenth-century America was shocked more easily: a neighbor's illicit affair was often the biggest thrill in town.

THAT WAS THEN, THIS IS NOW: In the 1932 cult film *Freaks*, the bearded lady falls in love with the "human skeleton" and wants to have his baby. Today, a bearded lady might be called the more politically correct "follicularly challenged." (The human skeleton would be called "nourishment challenged.") There is fortunately no place for "freaks" in today's more sensitive and tolerant American culture. The very idea of making them a spectacle is repugnant, especially in a time when otherness is more often celebrated and encouraged.

HYPOTHETICAL USAGE IN A SENTENCE BY THE OLD AND SETTLED: "Just because I'd like you to help me wash the dishes every now and then doesn't mean I'm a bearded lady or some other sort of freak." —Your grandmother, talking to her second husband, in about 1923

BETAMAX

A
DOOMED
TECHNOLOGY

TIMELINE: Betamax was a videocassette format that competed with VHS throughout most of the 1980s, but by 1988, it had lost the "format war" and its manufacturer, Sony, discontinued it.

INSPIRED GUESS BY TODAY'S YOUNG AND RESTLESS: A new breakfast cereal.

THE ANCIENT TRUTH: Betamax was a technology for playing, recording, and shooting videos. The "beta" part of its name comes from a Japanese word for signal transmission and references the similarity in shape between the way the tape was transported through the machine and the Greek letter "beta" or β. In Japan, where it was first developed in 1976, young people will be more familiar with Betamax because the technology there persisted until the early 2000s. Today's college students may be aware of the videotape format known as VHS—Betamax's

spirited competitor in the 1980s—but they consider it a relic of a time before the advent of digital video. At their colleges or universities, they may occasionally spy an old VHS player or perhaps find one in the attic or basement of their homes. Yet if VHS is an old format, Betamax is an "ancient" one. If it were still "alive" today in the sense of vast commercial usage, it would only be thirty-five years old! But it died a tragically early death in the United States, for it came out via Sony in 1977 and was discontinued in 1988.

Both VHS and Betamax were pioneers in the field of video recording. The devices provided a way for amateur, at-home users to create and present moving images. The affordable technology also made it possible for average, middle-class Americans to watch movies on their own TV sets, rather than having costly film projectors and white screens set up in their living rooms. Indeed, American consumers faced a dilemma back in the '80s: Betamax or VHS? Which one should they buy? American purchasers consulted clerks at Sears department stores, where Betamax players and camcorders were sold, for advice as though they were in touch with the Oracle at Delphi. Many of the clerks said "Beta," and despite the speed with which Betamax became obsolete, people had good reasons to believe they were right. Betamax featured a lighter machine and a sharper image. Beta machines also didn't waste as much tape space as VHS did. But inventors were slow to develop Beta into a single-unit camcorder, for which customers yearned, and it was more expensive to mass produce. Unfortunately, one could transfer Beta onto VHS but not vice versa.

THAT WAS THEN, THIS IS NOW: Betamax has lost the format war not once but twice: first to the more easily mass-produced VHS tape, and then altogether as videotape was rendered obsolete by the DVD.

DVD hath conquered all—except that it too is now falling prey to the higher-resolution Blu-ray disc and the convenience of Internet-based streaming like Netflix. Today it's only old adults who say, "Let's watch a film" on TV. Film, tape: all the "hard stuff" has been replaced by "digital." But let's not forget the days when, in order to watch a movie, you actually had to handle those ancient and terribly low-tech tangible things called cassettes.

In retrospect, the days of video recorders and players seem prehistoric. Imagine having to worry about keeping low-tech dust covers on machines so their inner parts didn't become damaged. Yet these were also revolutionary times. You could record *Oprah* in the afternoon and watch her after you got home from work—it was just a matter of getting the latchkey kids to set the machine when they got home from school. If that failed, you could always figure out how to use the timer on the machine before you went to work. The kids weren't always so reliable, but the stakes were high when it came to whether you got to watch *Oprah* or *Donahue* after a day of toil.

HYPOTHETICAL USAGE IN A SENTENCE BY THE OLD AND SETTLED:

"After I retire, I hope you will at least treat me as VHS, old but still occasionally reliable, and not as Betamax, utterly obsolete." —A man of about sixty-three, speaking pleadingly to his children, in about 1995

#11 BEULAH THE BUZZER

TIME'S UP

TIMELINE: *Truth or Consequences* was a popular radio and TV program for nearly fifty years. Beulah was a familiar feature on the show alongside the legendary host Bob Barker from 1956 to 1975.

INSPIRED GUESS BY TODAY'S YOUNG AND RESTLESS: Name for a pet bee.

THE ANCIENT TRUTH: Beulah was the name of the flatulent-sounding "time's up" buzzer on a long-running game show called *Truth or Consequences*, which aired on the radio from 1940 to 1957. It was the first game show ever aired on the new medium of television. As a TV game, it was popular on two major networks (CBS and NBC) and went into profitable syndication well into the late 1980s. Among its early hosts was Bob Barker, who later became a television icon as the longtime emcee of *The Price Is Right*. Barker is less renowned for *Truth or Consequences*, but TV viewers with a long enough memory—and sufficient marbles remaining in their noggins—will remember that they first met the young Barker on "*T or C*." In fact, it may have been Barker who coined the buzzer's name of Beulah.

Naming an inanimate object was consistent with the pervasive foolishness of the show. The game began with the emcee bringing on contestants and asking them a question they had to answer before Beulah buzzed to signal their time was up. In radio times, the questions were sent in by audience members and included "What starts with *T*, ends with *T*, and is full of tea?" (a teapot) and "How many times does a clock strike the hour in twenty-four hours?" (156). If contestants could not answer in time, the emcee would inform them they had not told "the truth" and thus must pay "the consequences." The zany consequences might entail traveling around the small stage on a unicycle but failing to master it in front of millions of people. The audience would laugh in an uproar. Unbeknownst to them until a bit later, one of the contestants was in fact a professional cyclist. Thus the audience got a "twofer": they got to laugh at the contestant's antics and enjoy the show of the pro. Beulah, it seems, brought great tidings of joy and amusement after all. But despite the success of the radio program, it was not until TV that Beulah made her debut and became the most famous—perhaps the *only* famous—buzzer in history.

In fact, *Truth or Consequences* sent a lot of different messages every time it was on: that Americans are good sports, that Americans are commercially ingenious people (contestants got prizes such as new slacks with expanding waistlines), that America is both a land of plenty *and* a land of limberness (the noncyclist contestant was rather overweight while the cyclist was very lithe), and, above all, that in America, consequences have an excellent chance to be cheery ones.

On *Truth or Consequences*, Beulah's buzz never portended a melancholy outcome. Bob Barker would sign off by hoping that "all your consequences are happy ones." Beulah, could she have spoken, would surely have agreed.

Shows in which Americans get to poke fun at other Americans have long been popular. There was the old *Candid Camera*. Its heyday of popularity was 1960–1967, and, like *Truth or Consequences*, continued on cable after it left network. But its format was much more popular and its programmatic life much longer, as it continued well into the '90s. *Candid Camera* specialized in practical jokes, such as thinly tethered wallets left on the sidewalk for unsuspecting people to try to pick up, only to find them scampering away, seemingly on their own. There is *America's Funniest Home Videos*, which frequently displays the screwups and dysfunctions of well-meaning families trying to have a swim or a cookout or a playground outing, where stuff goes wrong to the delight of those sitting comfortably at home. There is a minimal cruelty beneath these formulas, and that is probably why *Truth or Consequences* always leavened the ritual altruistically, with family reunions and, in its radio version, a year's supply of Duz detergent.

THAT WAS THEN, THIS IS NOW: In many ways, *Truth or Consequences* was a harbinger of what we call "reality TV" today. It put ordinary people in extraordinary situations, and audiences got to see how they responded. *Truth or Consequences* might reveal how a man reacted when unexpectedly reunited with his long-lost best friend, while *Survivor* would reveal how a woman reacted if voted off the island. While there is obviously a big difference between happy reunion and melancholy exile, an unscripted and spontaneous quality pertains to both—and this is the subtle media kinship between *Truth or Consequences* and *Survivor*.

HYPOTHETICAL USAGE IN A SENTENCE BY THE OLD AND SETTLED:

"Beulah the Buzzer has said your time is up and consequences must be paid." —Irate mother named Beulah in 1960 speaking to a teenage son at midnight, one hour after his curfew

#12

BILLY SUNDAY

A TRAIL OF SAWDUST

TIMELINE: Billy Sunday's professional heyday was principally in the 1920s.

INSPIRED GUESS BY TODAY'S YOUNG AND RESTLESS: A special dessert for Billy's birthday.

THE ANCIENT TRUTH: Billy Sunday was *the* great superstar evangelist of the early twentieth century and one of the biggest American celebrities of the time. In the 1920s, that decade of both flappers and piety, he was even more famous than **Aimee Semple McPherson**. By the time his career was over, he had reached well over a million souls (though perhaps some of them he reached two or three times), and millions more read of him in the paper. He was an angel in a suit and tie.

He was born William Sunday in 1862 in Iowa and was orphaned before his eleventh birthday. But he always seemed preternaturally industrious, neat, disciplined, and clean, even as a young man. He said the orphanages taught him these positive qualities, but it seems he really taught himself. In 1883, he became a big-league baseball player with the Chicago White Stockings, but he found Christ (or rather, Christ found him). On an 1887 summer's day in Chicago, he was inspired by a sidewalk brass band playing old Protestant hymns like "There Is a Fountain Filled with Blood" and "What a Friend We Have in Jesus." He gave up the occasional alcoholic drink and his habit of taking the Lord's name in vain. He went to work for a traveling evangelist—and so neat and hardworking was Sunday that by 1893, he was promoted to the preacher's assistant. He listened each night to the boss's sermonic techniques. Soon he began to study the Bible with an eye toward preaching, which he came to know thoroughly, in order to draw inspiration for his sermons. In these homilies, the literal virginity of Mary and factual resurrection of Jesus were as guaranteed as suspenders and corsets at an Iowa family reunion. By 1896, Billy Sunday, the old ballplayer, became a full-time preacher. He had decided to go to bat for Jesus.

A powerful public speaker and performer, Sunday quickly became America's most influential evangelist. In the early 1900s, long before electric amplifiers, he had to depend on his booming baritone to be heard. Early in his career, Sunday set up canvas tents to accommodate his large crowds, but after a big snowstorm destroyed one in a town in Colorado, he began to insist that the towns build temporary wooden tabernacles if they wanted to hear him preach. In 1909, in Joplin, Missouri, good men of the Lord spent fifty days constructing one prior to the great evangelist's advent upon the town.

Other towns did likewise. These were like barn raisings, and they were the quintessence of warm, righteous Protestant cooperation, complete with hardy men in shirtsleeves doing the lifting and raising, lemonade and pimento cheese sandwiches prepped by the ladies, and maybe a pickup baseball game for the kids to distract themselves. A Billy Sunday tabernacle, when completed, was a point of pride and served as a status symbol for the town. The town could reuse the tabernacle in the future for church revivals. Soon Billy began visiting larger and larger towns, even the big cities. His hardworking wife Nell finally agreed to leave the kids with a nanny so she could join her husband on the road. Together they developed a sort of Billy Sunday Inc., complete with advanced Bible teachers who would show up a week before Billy and conduct daily classes down at the tabernacle and the churches to maximize the great preacher's visit, which might last a month if the town were big enough.

These wooden tabernacles had sawdust sprinkled on the floor to muffle the shuffling of excited feet and cover the dusty, dirty floors. Those who accepted Sunday's invitation to acknowledge Jesus as their personal savior thus "hit the sawdust trail" down the aisle to the pulpit. His song leader even told members of the congregation how to muffle their sneezes in order to be silent for the Lord.

But even if he stayed only a night or two, he could thrill the congregants by proclaiming "what a spell the Devil casts upon the Church these days" or quipping that "going to church no more makes you a Christian than going to the garage makes you a car."

This was typical of Billy Sunday's attitude. His goal was not to prop up churches as organizations—his goal was to save individual souls, in church and out.

Sunday's celebrity status led to friendships with presidents and movie stars. As conservative preachers go, he was considered progressive. He was indispensably influential in getting Prohibition approved, and in 1917, he supported the United States going to war against Germany—but unlike a lot of fundamentalist Protestants, he was not prejudiced against Catholics or Unitarians. He tried to bridge the hostility between black and white.

Old age and illness finally got the best of him, and by the mid-1930s, his heyday was already behind him. His sermons continued to pass, sometimes quite brilliantly, as American entertainment. But he couldn't compete with movies and radio and never bothered to adapt to either. If he had, maybe he could have reached a million souls a *night*. Above all, the availability of radio and movies made a "night out at the tent revival" a less appealing proposition, and Sunday's audiences dwindled. His influence continued to wane over time. He had banked a lot of his prestige on Prohibition, but it became known as a failed experiment. The nation was becoming more urban and well educated; the old rural fundamentalism was starting to die. Sunday was an ardent "rugged individual" Republican, but by 1930, that idea had become discredited by the Depression. Billy Sunday died in 1935.

THAT WAS THEN, THIS IS NOW: Today Billy Sunday would be seen as a highly emotional and intense orator, much too hot and intrusive for the small TV living room, not to mention the laptop screen. No longer is our culture Bible-centered. But Billy Sunday is worth remembering for an era in which, to reach a million people, you had to travel.

Today, millions can be reached in an instant, thanks to the twenty-four-hour news cycle and social media. Let us hope that what is said is also worth listening to.

HYPOTHETICAL USAGE IN A SENTENCE BY THE OLD AND SETTLED:
"Reverend Jensen is no Billy Sunday. Jensen is boring, and it's a good thing too, because sometimes I need to doze in church." —Someone named Hilda Albert, speaking in about 1936 in Dayton, Ohio

BUCKY BEAVER

IN THE TEETH OF HISTORY

#13

TIMELINE: Ipana was a popular toothpaste brand in the United States from 1901 to 1979, and Bucky was the brand's singing icon in the 1950s and '60s.

INSPIRED GUESS BY TODAY'S YOUNG AND RESTLESS: Wasn't he a character on a *Ren and Stimpy* episode?

THE ANCIENT TRUTH: Bucky Beaver was the 1950s commercial mascot for Ipana toothpaste, which first appeared on the market around the turn of the century and had become a leading brand in the United States by the 1920s (it continued to be one until the late 1970s). The toothpaste was known for its wintergreen taste and featured sodium fluoride to prevent cavities. Manufactured by Bristol-Myers Squibb, the company was making so much money in pharmaceuticals by the '70s that it felt it could stop supporting Ipana even if sales dropped as a result. However, the brand remained popular in places such as Turkey, and in 2009 even came back as a "retro brand" in Canada. In the United States, it is largely forgotten. It has no cultural currency at all. The fact that computer spell-checkers flag "Ipana" as a misspelled or unknown word is a possible clue to its present obscurity.

Bucky existed to sell Ipana. In a typical commercial, Bucky, with his prominent front teeth, would combat the mustachioed and villainous "Mr. Tooth Decay." Then Bucky would sing his patented and triumphant jingle, "Brusha, brusha, brusha/with the new Ipana/with the brand new flavor/it's dandy for your teeth." As late as 1978, one of the girls from the Pink Ladies high school clique sings the jingle during a sleepover in the film *Grease*, an acclaimed musical. Is such replication the highest form of flattery? Maybe it is, but 1978 was nearly forty years ago—and no wide audience has heard from Bucky since then.

Initially, Ipana never made any quasi-scientific claims about its effectiveness. To drive sales, it depended on its sweet taste, the appeal of Bucky to children of all ages, and the gratitude of older Americans (who were happy to have toothpaste after generations of fast-rotting teeth and dentures). In time, though, Americans grew savvier, demanding proof of effectiveness, which provided Ipana's competitor, Procter & Gamble's Crest, with an opportunity. Crest stepped in and announced that its brand had a special ingredient called "Fluoristan," which could prevent tooth decay, as though it were some sort of research breakthrough. In fact, Fluoristan was just stannous fluoride, a derivation of what Ipana had. But Crest wasn't done. The company also elicited an endorsement from the American Dental Association, while Ipana continued to rely on the goofy charms of an animated beaver. As a result, Crest replaced Ipana as America's number-one brand. Bristol-Myers Squibb, by then pioneering drugs for chemo-therapy and relief of anxiety, decided to discontinue Ipana, whose market share was declining, in 1979. Bucky could defeat Mr. Tooth Decay—but not Mr. Obscurity.

The history of Ipana suggests that its place in American culture is more heterogeneous and darker than the silliness of Bucky might suggest. Allen Ginsberg, the once-scandalous Beat poet, did market research for Ipana. No commercial product can be all bad if it can claim, as part of its lineage, a man who wrote "I saw the best minds of my generation destroyed by madness, starving hysterical naked,/dragging themselves through the negro streets at dawn looking for an angry fix..." What Bucky would make of such disturbing sentiments is hard to imagine.

THAT WAS THEN, THIS IS NOW: Bucky's commercials were silly, but that's not significant in and of itself, for most commercials today are silly too—even if they are expressed not by beavers with protruding canines, but by day geckos with cockney accents. While frivolous commercials continue to sell insurance (and beer and other products), we now live in an era where consumers are better informed and seek out evidence of product effectiveness. Bucky by himself just can't quite hack it any more. The GEICO gecko exists in a scheme of comparative shopping—something Bucky was never part of.

HYPOTHETICAL USAGE IN A SENTENCE BY THE OLD AND SETTLED:

"I no longer consider Bucky Beaver the best mind of my generation."
—What Allen Ginsberg *should* have said when he decided to quit working for Ipana in order to become the great Beat bard of New York and San Francisco

CHARLIE CHAN

A MULTICULTURAL SUPER SLEUTH

TIMELINE: Author Earl Derr Biggers first created the Charlie Chan character in 1919. The first Chan film was a 1926 silent, and the films continued through 1981.

INSPIRED GUESS BY TODAY'S YOUNG AND RESTLESS: An online bulletin board where visitors can post images depicting Asian culture.

THE ANCIENT TRUTH: Charlie Chan was a fictional, popular Chinese American detective, prominently featured in books, movies, radio, television, and comic strips during the 1930s and '40s (much less so after that, though the last Chan film was in the early 1980s). The idea for Charlie Chan was first conceived in 1919, when an author with the unlikely name of Earl Derr Biggers went to Hawaii and eventually met a skilled Chinese American detective named Chang Apana. Biggers based his character

Charlie Chan on this real-life figure. The Chan novels were a successful pulp mystery series, and the character quickly became popular.

The reassuring, crime-busting Chan served as the anti–Yellow Peril, the name for a stereotype of the demonic Chinese villain Fu Manchu. This was the negative image of Asian men most feared by whites. Chan, by contrast, was depicted as admirable and benevolent. His exciting adventures took fans from London to Paris, Egypt to Broadway, and even to the circus and opera. It was not until the 1930s that the series became internationally famous with films starring a variety of actors. In particular, the Swedish actor Warner Oland (who also claimed some Mongolian heritage) truly put his mark on the character. But despite the popularity of the character, many people chafed at the depiction of Charlie Chan, believing him to be a racist portrayal of an Asian American.

The character appeared in the film *Charlie Chan and the Dragon Lady* as late as 1981, but by that time, ethnic sensitivities were so rife that the film was opposed by a group with the most decorous acronym CAN (Coalition of Asians to Nix). As a result, the film performed poorly in the box office.

Indeed, Chan was always depicted as polite, brilliant, observant, and courtly. But he was also exceedingly bland and deferential to authority (even to the murderers he exposed). Charlie Chan is inescapably an ethnic stereotype, and any such stereotype denies the full complexity and humanity of an individual. Charlie Chan's courtesy and brilliance are perhaps less important than his obsequiousness. He seems to exist, above all, not to threaten his nervous Caucasian masters!

And perhaps most offensively of all, Chan was always played by white actors and spoke in Pidgin English.

Still, we must be wary not to oversimplify. Chan's halting English is contrasted by the much more fluent American English of his second-generation Chinese American son, often played by actor Keye Luke. And his courtly deference is part of an act to confuse the crooks. Chan seems to lack any threatening qualities so villains would seem to have little reason to fear him. This is also a clever plot, not just a cultural stereotype. Charlie Chan, then, was both ethnic stereotype and admirable character. As a fictional character, it was impossible to disentangle the two.

THAT WAS THEN, THIS IS NOW: What would today's young folks think of Chan? They'd find the films creakingly slow. A generation impatient with getting a laptop booted up would grind its teeth waiting for Charlie to do anything. Today's youngsters would see in Chan an Asian character they would not recognize. They would see his politeness, intelligence, and seeming obedience, but having no experience and little background in the Yellow Peril, they wouldn't be able to decode the meaning of Chan for the '30s and '40s, when he was at once an expression of three regrettable Western attitudes toward Asians: a feeling of superiority over them, a grudging admiration of their cleverness, and a need to believe that their cunning would always be harmless to the great majority of the white race. During that time period, the majority of white audiences in the United States thought of themselves as superior to Asians—yet they were simultaneously worried about the military threat from the Japanese. Today's millennials would mostly just be bored by Charlie. They're more likely to visit Beijing itself on a cheap flight found on the Internet than to consider Charlie Chan as true entertainment.

HYPOTHETICAL USAGE IN A SENTENCE BY THE OLD AND SETTLED:

"That waiter reminds me of Charlie Chan so much that I wonder if there's a killer in the house." —Your grandfather talking to your grandmother in a restaurant in Colorado Springs, Colorado, around 1940

CHARLIE McCARTHY

AND NOW A WORD FROM THE DUMMY

#15

TIMELINE: Ventriloquist Edgar Bergen and his sidekick Charlie McCarthy appeared regularly on the radio and TV from 1937 to 1971.

INSPIRED GUESS BY TODAY'S YOUNG AND RESTLESS: The younger brother of Jenny McCarthy, who cohosts that daytime talk show *The View*.

THE ANCIENT TRUTH: Charlie McCarthy was the chief sidekick of a famous ventriloquist named Edgar Bergen. The smart-aleck young Charlie, with his monocle, top hat, and formal black coat, became the most famous wooden man in the United States. Bergen's technical art, on the other hand, left something to be desired. Audience members and even viewers at home could clearly see his lips moving, a motion he unsuccessfully tried to hide by getting the audience to focus on Charlie.

That's because Bergen had mainly been a radio

star from the 1930s on. Except for the small live studio audience, he hadn't needed to worry about moving his lips during his early career. His secret was not in his technical skill as a ventriloquist but in his hilarious material and his dummy characters that cut such vivid profiles into the imaginations of listeners that they seemed real. Charlie always came off as a patrician swell, and his aristocratic hauteur and roving eye for the ladies were ever on display.

For nearly twenty years, Bergen presided over one of the most popular radio programs of the '30s, '40s, and '50s, known as *The Chase and Sanborn Hour* (Chase and Sanborn was a bestselling coffee). He and Charlie also emceed the game show *Who Do You Trust?* on CBS from 1956 to 1957. (They were succeeded by a young Johnny Carson.) Yet Bergen's most important place in American social history is traceable to Halloween 1938, when those listening decided to switch to a program by director and actor Orson Welles during a musical interlude on Bergen's show. Welles was infamously dramatizing a Martian attack on the United States in his program *War of the Worlds*, but Bergen listeners who came into the show out of context thought it was the real thing. Thousands panicked, many of them fleeing in their cars. Such hysteria could be fairly blamed on Charlie McCarthy, who would have been smart-alecky enough to enjoy the entire snafu and delighted to take the credit for it.

THAT WAS THEN, THIS IS NOW: Charlie had sibling dummies, including Mortimer Snerd and Effie Klinker. Charlie, Mortimer, and Effie were all characterizations of American stereotypes: the snobbish swell, the funny half-wit, and the sexually ravenous old maid. But such types have passed from the American scene and with them any chance that they will ever be funny again. Even ventriloquism doesn't seem all that attractive any longer. In the present age, when we can make anyone talk with digital equipment, throwing one's voice seems a little low-tech. Today Charlie resides in a glass case at the Smithsonian Museum in Washington, DC. He's a historical relic of a far different time.

HYPOTHETICAL USAGE IN A SENTENCE BY THE OLD AND SETTLED:
"Unlike Charlie McCarthy, you're a dummy *without* wit." —Mabel Breeland, speaking to her besieged husband Grady, in 1944

#16 CIGARETTE GIRL

A BEAUTY WITH A TRAY

TIMELINE: Cigarette girls were a fixture in American nightclubs in the 1920s through the '60s.

INSPIRED GUESS BY TODAY'S YOUNG AND RESTLESS: An underage teen addicted to nicotine.

THE ANCIENT TRUTH: The cigarette girl typically wore an above-the-knee dress, buttressed by a rigid, steel-like petticoat. It was usually red and black. Sometimes she wore a hat, such as a shorter top hat for ladies. An hourglass figure was a matter of some considerable emphasis farther up, and fishnet stockings and stiletto heels adorned her pretty legs below. It was quite the get-up: not demure by any means, but never really considered vulgar either. Consider it a matter of tasteful pulchritude.

Equally important was a large, flat tray hung from her neck and supported by her hands. On this tray rested mostly regimented cigarettes (Pall Malls,

Old Golds, and **Lucky Strikes**), but also some cigars and maybe, in the 1950s, lighted yo-yos or trinkets. Sometimes she was called the candy girl because she was, of course, the proverbial eye candy before that phrase became popular.

Such a visual treat was a fixture of Hollywood media too. In films set in nightclubs, she was only good to swell a scene. She would come on-screen and ask maybe Joan Crawford and her latest boyfriend (almost always a bad choice, for Joan was never wise in her selection of men) if they'd like a cigarette. She would ask in a silky, come-hither voice, "Cigars, cigarettes?" and then move on to the next table and out of the movie. The cig girl would wear high heels, as though to suggest that she would never, ever speed away with her bounty but offer it reliably and slowly, even sensually.

The cigarette girl still exists in a few nightclubs in Las Vegas, and there was even a 2009 indie film called *Cigarette Girl* about a crazed young woman who has such terrible weed withdrawal that she goes on a delusional murderous rage. Here, the cigarette girl smokes a pistol as much as a Camel.

And they were *girls*. They offered, as sexy proto-mothers to grown-up *boys*, the wrapped tobacco, capable of being lit and ingested into the adult male's eagerly awaiting lungs. The cigarettes were complimentary, and the girls would even light them with gold or silver lighters. Cigarettes were part of the cover charge—one of those freebies that you knew you've paid for but that you thought you were getting for zilch, rather like the "free" continental breakfast at today's motels.

Your Kents and Philip Morrises tasted a lot better accompanied by the afterimage of the comely lass who had given them to you.

THAT WAS THEN, THIS IS NOW: Why has the cigarette girl become an artifact of a previous time? People who go to nightclubs nowadays are likely to be greeted with no-smoking signs; they're more likely to enjoy lobster bisque with a single glass of chardonnay, watch the show, and get up early for jogging the next day—a feat made possible by non-carcinogenic lungs. And calling grown women "girls" is condescending. Both feminism and the health craze have rendered the cigarette girl a thing of the past.

HYPOTHETICAL USAGE IN A SENTENCE BY THE OLD AND SETTLED: "This is not a nightclub, and I'm not your cigarette girl." —A late 1960s feminist speaking at a Vermont commune about gender equality

COLLECT CALL

HOPING FOR GENEROSITY

TIMELINE: Collect calls were popular, if expensive, telephone practices in the 1920s through the '50s, when the advent of area codes and direct dialing began.

INSPIRED GUESS BY TODAY'S YOUNG AND RESTLESS: It must be the old name for a conference call, in which a *collection* of people would converse together by phone.

THE ANCIENT TRUTH: A collect phone call was one placed by the caller but charged to the recipient. Another relevant phrase was "reverse the charges," by which one could call a stingy uncle long-distance, pretend it was an emergency, and then have the operator request that "the charges be reversed," resulting in a "free" call. Beginning in the 1920s, long-distance calls were considered a big deal. They were both costly and rare, and one had to go through the operator to make them. Depending on the distance from which the call was made and the time of the conversation, a single collect call might cost as much as ten dollars, which in 1950 would equal ninety-eight 2014 dollars. As a result, the recipients of collect calls tended to be family members, close friends, or someone who had been sufficiently bribed or blackmailed!

For example, a caller from Bison City, North Dakota, would waver between pretension and anxiety as he declared, "I'd like to make a long-distance telephone call to Tyler, Texas," after the operator said, "Number, please." Then the caller would provide the number to the operator, but prior to 1947, there were no area codes. Rather, the caller would say "PL 70945 in Tyler, Texas" (the PL would stand for the exchange code, which in this case might be "Plaza"), and the operator would need to figure out how to plug particular wires into the proper outlets to connect the two phone lines. Unlike today's largely instantaneous and automated process, this method was intricate and often took time. Sometimes the call would not go through, and the caller would be invited to try again later. Once the operator connected with the receiving party, she would say: "I have a collect long-distance call from a Buff Tyson in Bison City, North Dakota, for a Ebenezer Z. Scrooge in Tyler. Will you accept?" If the recipient said yes, the costs would be charged to *him*.

The phones themselves were quite heavy, often made of a leaden material called **Bakelite**. The dial mechanism was sticky and reluctant, as though to create a sort of tacit guilt in performing the operation and thus spending the money. Extremely rural areas had "party lines," on which you were assigned a particular ringing pattern (for example, two short rings, one long) that indicated that it was you whom the caller wished to reach and not your neighbor with whom you shared the line. Sometimes, when you picked up the phone, you found your neighbor already on the line and in the middle of a conversation, and you were not supposed to listen in (though you often did). But if there was an emergency, if you needed to get Doc Adams out right away for a diarrheic pig, then you said so and generally got the line right away.

Party lines were for "hicks." Collect calls were for wealthy sophisticates, but even so, middle-class people also made them, though sparingly. They were mostly for holidays or birthdays, as well as the occasional emergency ("Aunt Martha has had a stroke, but they think she'll get well"). A collect call—whether made in an unusual moment of joy or an unforgettable instance of shame or fear—nearly always had drama surrounding it. Even phone calls in general could be riveting in the right context. A famous 1948 film, *Sorry, Wrong Number*, is still terrifying today. Even better, try watching it on your iPhone.

THAT WAS THEN, THIS IS NOW: Phone calls are rarely thrillers anymore, and nowadays even the concept of long distance has evaporated. No one thinks much about dialing direct across country or even internationally, because there are all sorts of budget plans to make such calls quite affordable. The only place these days from which a collect call is required is jail: they are the only sorts of calls inmates are allowed to make. And a phone, once thought an instrument for talking to someone who was not in the next room, is now a portable encyclopedia, a camera, and much more. People used to simply talk on phones. Now they can watch movies on them. And even that doesn't seem like a big deal.

HYPOTHETICAL USAGE IN A SENTENCE BY THE OLD AND SETTLED:

"Today is Jimmy's first college class, so let's sit down, have a gin fizz, and wait for the almost-certain collect call asking for bus fare home."
—James Sherrill Sr. speaking to his wife Agnes in September 1946

COPYBOY

A SPRINTER IN THE NEWSROOM

 # 18

TIMELINE: A copyboy was essential to American print journalism from the late nineteenth century until the 1980s, when the internal transmission of stories became primarily electronic.

INSPIRED GUESS BY TODAY'S YOUNG AND RESTLESS: A new app that maximizes the speed of computerized cut and paste.

THE ANCIENT TRUTH: A copyboy was a staple of newspaper city rooms until the advent of the digital age. His essential job was "human messenger": to take copies of reporters' stories to other parts of the newspaper operation, such as editing, layout, and print setting. During this time period, newspaper stories were often created in carbon copy form. Carbon copies—the acronym "cc" still survives on email—refers to a way of copying paper documents that depended on the pressure of typewriters, pens, and pencils and the capacity of carbon-based ink to create impressions called "duplicate" (two copies plus the original). Reporters were sometimes called "ink-stained wretches," first because they used so much ink to write their tales, and later, once typing was in vogue, because they handled so much carbon paper that the ink would bleed onto their hands. After 1900, very few reporters hand-wrote their stories—typewriters were in vogue—but the typewritten stories still needed to follow a specific process. The stories went to an editor and then to make-up or composition, where the entire newspaper was laid out. Finally, the newspaper was sent off to the printers, who set the type.

> Thanks to the copyboy and an efficient process for the division of labor, the newspaper became a well-oiled machine. The presence of copyboys gave reporters the freedom to gather their information and write their stories without distraction. In his heyday, the copyboy was well-nigh crucial to his city paper.

Reporters would yell, "Copy!" and the copyboy would come running for the hand-off. He (or occasionally she) would then race to the next department to deliver the story to the next pair of eyes. Various drudges in the newspaper business who often stood higher than the wretched reporter would decide whether the story would go into the paper, how long it would be, how it was to be laid out, and on what page it would appear. But despite this complex process, the linchpin was quite simple: an ordinary lad receiving something and getting it to others—fast.

THAT WAS THEN, THIS IS NOW: In today's digital era, the copyboy is not required. Reporters may still be wretches, but they rarely have ink on their hands. Journalists now primarily process their stories on computers and email them to their editors. The copyboy has gone with the wind, which has also blown away carbon paper and perhaps even daily, tangible newspapers themselves. Some major dailies have already become online only, and the reporter is being replaced by millions of less-costly bloggers, who also gather information and break up-to-the-minute stories. Perhaps the newspapers of the future will be delivered only in Braille to the blind. Everyone else will read online.

HYPOTHETICAL USAGE IN A SENTENCE BY THE OLD AND SETTLED: "Unless you want to grow up to be a forty-year-old copyboy, you'd better study harder, Jimmy." —James Dromgoole's father, speaking to his son about his terrible grades, 1939

#19 CRIME OF THE CENTURY

UNLUCKY LINDY AND JFK

TIMELINE: A term to describe horrific crimes, primarily used throughout the twentieth century.

INSPIRED GUESS BY TODAY'S YOUNG AND RESTLESS: Whatever crime Nancy Grace is covering this week.

THE ANCIENT TRUTH: If you ask today's young people to describe "the crime of the century," they might answer with "9/11." Although the terrorist attacks on New York City and Washington, DC, on September 11, 2001, were devastating, the expression "crime of the century" actually predates the terrible event. It's a term that originated in the twentieth century. So what *was* the "crime of the century," and how did the term arise? There is no person to whom the term can be first attributed; rather, it's an idiomatic term rooted in repeated usage. Any sensational crime may attract the label, but in actuality there were only two truly plausible candidates for "crime of the century" in twentieth-century America. To qualify as a "crime of the century," we believe the crime needs to meet the following criteria:

- *the outrageous slaughter of an innocent person, a famous person, or both*
- *blaring headlines and the most spongelike of media coverage*
- *endless theories about who did it and why*

These standards explain why the only two cases deserving of the "crime of the century" label are the kidnapping and murder of Charles Lindbergh's infant son in New Jersey in 1932 and the assassination of President Kennedy in Dallas in 1963.

- *Charles August Lindbergh Jr., son of the idolized aviator, was kidnapped and murdered in March 1932, allegedly by a Bronx carpenter named Bruno Richard Hauptmann. Little Charles tragically came to be a stand-in for his father, for to strike at Little Charles, "the Lone Eaglet," was to strike at Big Charles, "the Lone Eagle." One journalist, H. L. Mencken, called it the greatest story since the crucifixion of Christ. Numerous theories have been propounded about the subject. Some of them allege the most likely truth: that Bruno Hauptmann alone stole the Eaglet for ransom, killed him, and hid his body, convincing the Lindberghs through letters that he was still alive and collecting the ransom money, which was finally traced to Hauptmann. In 1935, he was convicted of the crime and executed for it. Other theorists argue that Hauptmann was innocent (or guilty of no more than extortion) and that the real culprit was a gang that had inside help from a Lindbergh employee, or even that Lindbergh himself had accidentally killed the little Eaglet and had concocted the kidnapping hoax as a cover-up. As with the Kennedy murder, hypotheses abound.*

❧ *The thirty-fifth president of the United States, John F. Kennedy, was assassinated in November 1963 while innocently riding, amid great cheer, in an open car in downtown Dallas. The media coverage was utterly saturating, especially during the period between the Friday of the killing and the Monday funeral: a long weekend in which Americans and world citizens alike did nothing but watch TV accounts of the grim event. The speculation and conspiracy theories about whether Lee Harvey Oswald acted alone may never end.*

These were terrible crimes and were further pockmarks on a century of world wars. Yet the phrase "crime of the century" has a subtle affirmative meaning. It's a tacit way of slapping the whole twentieth century on the back. For all that went wrong between 1901 and 2000, so much went right: the invention of cars, airplanes, telephones, radio, television, penicillin, the cure for polio, and computers, to name a few. There is no way to understand or experience the twentieth century without taking into account these technological "miracles." So in spite of the mass slaughters and great economic calamities caused by two world wars, there was a celebratory quality to the century, as though journalists decided to celebrate their new media by obliquely praising *even the magnitude of the century's crimes.*

THAT WAS THEN, THIS IS NOW: The term "crime of the century" is really a method of revisiting the twentieth century. But now, we have moved on, not only to a new century, but also a new millennium. As a result, familiarity with the horrific killings of the *last* century is being replaced with the crimes of *this* century, such as the Sandy Hook school murders in November 2012 or the Boston Marathon bombing in April 2013. The kidnapping of the Lindbergh baby was so long ago that it probably seems ho-hum to today's audience. On an even darker note, our culture is saturated with crime stories now, thanks in part to the twenty-four-hour news cycle. There are terrible crimes committed every day, but this is just one more bit of information on the data-rich Internet. Are we becoming so jaded that in the new millennium the term "crime of the century" will lose its currency and shock value?

HYPOTHETICAL USAGE IN A SENTENCE BY THE OLD AND SETTLED:

"Okay, I admit it: I ate the rest of the pound cake—the crime of the century, right?" —Anonymous, speaking defensively to his parents, in 1946

#20 DEWEY DEFEATS TRUMAN

OOPS!

TIMELINE: The original headline in the *Chicago Tribune* appeared the day after the November 1948 presidential election.

INSPIRED GUESS BY TODAY'S YOUNG AND RESTLESS: Uh, maybe the headline after a tennis match between a player named Truman and a player named Dewey. Weren't they Australians?

THE ANCIENT TRUTH: The *Chicago Tribune*'s gleeful headline happened to be premature—and completely wrong. An iconic photo from the day depicts a jovial President Harry S. Truman holding up the newspaper for the cameras after he had upset Governor Thomas Dewey. Truman did this not only to gloat over his unexpected victory, but also to stick it to the *Tribune*, a relentlessly and unashamedly Republican newspaper.

The *Tribune* could hardly be blamed for

expecting Dewey to win, though its management could be—and was—for its decidedly premature proclamation. Everyone thought Dewey would win. No one, or so the joke went, would admit having voted for Truman, so when the *Tribune* made its infamous mistake, there was a degree of public understanding. Conventional wisdom seemed to agree that Truman had seemed overmatched by his job. He was a partisan, sometimes bumbling little rooster: hardly the eloquent, charismatic Franklin Roosevelt, whom Truman had succeeded. Truman inherited some awful post–World War II repercussions, including the inflation that arose inevitably from the country's wartime economy. Anger over rising prices soared, regardless of which party one belonged to. Ultimately, the shift from a wartime to a peacetime nation was a painful transition, the sort the president always gets blamed for. Truman had never been to college and faced internal challenges from both parties, with Republicans blaming him for incompetence and his own Democrats blaming him for being both too conservative for its liberal wing and too liberal for its conservative wing. Meanwhile, the Republicans, having been shut out of power for fourteen years, had made a big comeback in the 1946 elections and became the dominant congressional party. The country seemed tired of the Democratic agenda of community and sacrifice that had steered the country through the Great Depression and World War II. Truman's opponent, the brave and resourceful prosecutor and governor of New York, seemed a credible candidate indeed.

The election seemed close for a while on that fateful November evening, with election returns showing Truman and Dewey running neck and neck. This was surprising in and of itself, but then Truman had run a scrappy campaign while Dewey spoke in uninspiring generalities. He seemed to be banking on the simple fact that he was not Harry Truman. But with the election still too close to call on that early November night in 1948, the *Tribune* decided that surely Dewey would win it and therefore went to press with this notorious headline. Besides, the *Tribune* wanted Dewey to win. Who could have predicted the greatest upset in American electoral history?

The Depression was over, and the war was won. It was time to kick back and enjoy life rather than having to worry about the next big crisis. The country longs for "normalcy, not nostrums," said Senator Warren G. Harding on his way to the White House in 1920. A similar mood resurfaced in 1948. That autumn, Republicans were optimistic about the election. Democrats were gloomy and wished they were not stuck with Truman. Even if Truman were president, he was only there by accident—and not for much longer.

THAT WAS THEN, THIS IS NOW: The famous photo of Truman holding up the incorrect *Tribune* headline still ranks as an iconic image of American political history. But in twenty or thirty years, there may not be any newspapers left, so future generations may ask, "What is that thing that man is holding up?"

HYPOTHETICAL USAGE IN A SENTENCE BY THE OLD AND SETTLED: "You say this machine can be fixed? What fantasy are you going to tell me next: that Dewey defeats Truman?" —A wife admonishing her cheapskate husband in 1949, after he insisted he could repair the washing machine himself

DING DONG SCHOOL

BEFORE
MR. ROGERS

TIMELINE: Miss Frances Horwich's *Ding Dong School* ran on NBC from 1952 to 1956.

INSPIRED GUESS BY TODAY'S YOUNG AND RESTLESS: The nickname for a special college program organized to tutor football players.

THE ANCIENT TRUTH: *Ding Dong School* was commercial television's noble attempt at educational broadcasting for children, the precursor to iconic programs such as *Sesame Street* and *Mister Rogers' Neighborhood*. *Ding Dong School* only lasted four years, after which the more commercially successful game show *The Price Is Right* replaced it.

Ding Dong School was the brainchild of Frances Horwich, the head of the education department at Chicago's Roosevelt University. For a few years (1954–1956), she was made head of all of NBC's children's programming and moved to New York, but after *Ding Dong School* was canceled in 1956, she went back to Chicago. Her fame was short-lived, but for millions of children, today in their sixties, she was as well-known as their rubber ducky toy.

Ding Dong School originated in Chicago, Illinois. It was part of the Chicago school of early TV: quiet, intimate, and uncanny. Although Chicago-based programming accounted for only 5 percent of early television content, it was by far the most innovative, based on an understanding that TV performers were "guests" in the viewer's living rooms and should behave accordingly. In live performances or perhaps on the big screen, performers might need to *entertain* children, but on television's small screen, it was believed to be more appropriate to *interact* with them.

"Miss Frances" Horwich embodied this belief. She was the quintessential gentle person, starting each show by ringing a bell and singing a little ditty. Thus did she beckon America's four- and five-year-olds. She would demonstrate how to fashion a turtle out of clay. She would read poems about shadows and the moon. She would not endorse toys that were even implicitly violent, such as cap pistols or miniature tanks. She would address the kids at home (as did Fred Rogers later) and then give them a chance to answer.

"Today is Friday. How do you plan to spend your weekend?" (Pause)
"Playing outdoors? Doesn't that sound like fun?" (Pause)
"I hope the weather is nice for you."

She was never a condescending or bossy schoolmarm. Miss Frances was able to inspire children to silence just by illustrating its virtues herself. For example, she would get a bowl of water, pour soap into it, and then with a bubble pipe, she would simply blow bubbles for her audience. She would say nothing—all was quiet on the bubble front—while the camera simply adored all the bubbles that came forth: big ones, little ones, quickly popping ones, and more enduring ones. Today's audience would probably feel impatience with this quiet gentleness, but once upon a time, we too were capable of being amazed by the simplest things and even, for a little while, able to sit quietly and just watch. She taught children that the world was a marvelous place, where there was always something new to notice if only they paid attention.

> Part of what made Miss Frances so successful on television is that she recognized that small children learn best through fun and delight—there's no telling five-year-olds, for instance, that they must learn something because they'll "need it some-day"! Miss Frances used everything at her disposal—from the performance of simple tricks to the reading of poetry—to engage and educate her young viewers.

Although *Ding Dong School* eventually acquired commercial sponsorship (Kix cereal), in the end, there weren't enough kids with shallow pockets to outweigh the number of adult ladies with deep purses, so in 1956, *Ding Dong School* was succeeded by *The Price Is Right*. This event suggests the rationale for PBS and *Sesame Street*, where outstanding programming is not required to submit to the vagaries of the consumer marketplace.

THAT WAS THEN, THIS IS NOW: Today's Generation Y takes public television for granted. They first learned about the letter Z on *Sesame Street* from Grover and were first reassured about their parents' divorce by Mr. Rogers. Children's programming has always been a part of their lives. They would look back, perhaps, on NBC's decision to go with *The Price Is Right* as ignoble. (Parents, sorry to lose thirty free minutes of babysitting each day, didn't like the replacement either!) Miss Frances surely thought so too. But what Gen Y might not fully understand is that in those early days of television, the commercial networks really did try to do some good for their young viewers. When they failed, public television and radio took up the slack. We should remember Miss Frances's *Ding Dong School* not just for what she did, but also for how her noble work paved the way for a revolution in children's programming—leading to wonderful, interactive shows like PBS's *Mister Rogers' Neighborhood* and *Sesame Street*, Nickelodeon's *Blue's Clues* and *Dora the Explorer*, and many more beloved examples.

HYPOTHETICAL USAGE IN A SENTENCE BY THE OLD AND SETTLED:

"You don't know how to make your own bubble water? I'd have thought you'd have learned that years ago on *Ding Dong School*." —Mr. Gerald Buckalew, speaking ironically to his ten-year-old son Eli, in 1963

DON AMECHE

RINGS  BELL

TIMELINE: Don Ameche was a film actor for nearly sixty years (in addition to his work in plays and TV and radio). His first film was released in 1935, and his last was released in 1993, just days before his death at age eighty-five.

INSPIRED GUESS BY TODAY'S YOUNG AND RESTLESS: The lead character in *The Godfather*.

THE ANCIENT TRUTH: Dominic Felix Amici, born of an Italian father and a Scotch-Irish German mother in Wisconsin in 1908, went on to become one of the most beloved and versatile actors of the twentieth century—stage, screen, radio, and TV. Don Ameche (as he was later called once his name had been scrubbed of its "ethnic" spelling) was always perceived as eminently American. Although he had thought of becoming an attorney, show business beckoned. He was in vaudeville during the '20s—when it was dying as a showbiz form—but by the '30s, he had attained stardom in Hollywood as the perfect American character: genial but flawed, smooth and suave with a few demons. Yet his most memorable role is that of a Scottish American: Alexander Graham Bell, the inventor of the telephone.

Ameche had a long career—he won an Oscar in his '80s for his role in *Cocoon*—and has a star on Hollywood's Walk of Fame. He was married to the same woman for fifty years and had six children. His likable nature continued until the end of his life. For example, the actress Jamie Lee Curtis once told Larry King that when Ameche, an octogenarian, had to say the F-word on camera, he apologized to everyone in the cast ahead of time.

When we think of great Hollywood biopics, we think of men of action: George C. Scott's General Patton, Robert De Niro's boxer Jake La Motta, even Russell Crowe's John Nash. Despite the challenge of making film biographies, some Hollywood producers believed that the film industry ought to be educational, so why not give the audience a little instruction in telephonic communication? The producers knew they had a ready-made audience in the '30s: sad-sacked by the Depression, moviegoers wanted good news, and civilization's great technologies certainly counted as such. Even if the economists had gone bust, we still had the scientists on our side!

Why was Ameche's portrayal in *The Story of Alexander Graham Bell* so notable? Partly because the flick itself is a convincingly weepy account of the trail from domestic tragedy (Bell's wife contracted scarlet fever at an early age and lost her hearing) to scientific triumph (he made it possible for millions to hear one another across long distances). Ameche brilliantly plays both the loving husband and the victorious inventor, as though his husbandly affections cannot be separated from his determination to create the telephone. He overacts a bit, but then it's such a compelling story, why not? And then the movie furnished Americans with years and years of quips like these: "Who invented the telephone? Why, Don Ameche, of course." And while it may be difficult to believe today, as a result of the popularity of Ameche's character, many Americans referred to the telephone as "the Ameche." No one will ever refer to a fighter jet as "the (Tom) Cruise" or a first-class passenger ship's cabin as "the (Kate) Winslet." Yet Don had such an impact on American culture that he is remembered as a unique actor in the annals of American show business.

THAT WAS THEN, THIS IS NOW: The 1930s saw two great biopics of scientists: *The Story of Alexander Graham Bell* (1939) and *The Story of Louis Pasteur* (1936). These were riveting tales about two major advances of the then-young twentieth century—the phone and vaccination. And what are some of the advances of the late twentieth century and the early part of the twenty-first? They include mathematical game theory and Facebook, so no wonder we have such biopics as *A Beautiful Mind* (about the mathematician John Nash) and *The Social Network* (about Facebook founder Mark Zuckerberg). Yet these newer films have a troubling edge that the two earlier ones do not. Nash was certifiably crazy for a while, and Zuckerberg's success is fraught with lawsuits and infighting. Today, even the late Steve Jobs—though we celebrate him for the genius from which we have all benefited—is known as having been a prickly, egotistical man. Bell and Pasteur were heroes in a way that our modern scientists and creators seem not to be. Perhaps today we have too much information—for better or worse— about the great geniuses of our time.

HYPOTHETICAL USAGE IN A SENTENCE BY THE OLD AND SETTLED:

"You're wanted on the Ameche. I think it's the maternity ward." —Your great-aunt speaking to your great-uncle, while giving him a frigid stare on January 8, 1951.

DO NOT FOLD, BEND, SPINDLE, OR MUTILATE

#23

A CARD GAME

TIMELINE: Punch cards were used throughout the twentieth century as a way of both recording and storing data. But by the 1960s, magnetic tape began to replace them.

INSPIRED GUESS BY TODAY'S YOUNG AND RESTLESS: Instructions given to kids about their Go Fish or Spoons cards.

THE ANCIENT TRUTH: Known as punch cards, Hollerith cards, or (much more famously) IBM cards, these pieces of stiff paper were the first sophisticated way to gather, tabulate, and store information. They are the prototype of contemporary computer programming, but whereas computer programs are "software" (a collection of instructions and code), the punch cards were a sort of "hardware," meaning you could physically touch them. Punch cards were about 7.5 inches

long, about 3 inches down, and about .007 inches thick. If anyone bent, folded, spindled (speared), or mutilated one, it became useless and the information was lost.

Punch cards are almost never used in American life today, with one recent exception being the Sparkler Filters Company of Conroe, Texas, which recorded transactions on a large 1948 computer that was so rare that the Computer History Museum of California tried to get the company to donate it. But punch cards are generally as rare today as telephone booths are for the current generation of youth. They may never see one, unless perhaps fourteen years ago they voted in Florida—where voter punch cards that were not punched all the way through ("hanging chads") created a serious problem for the 2000 Bush-Gore presidential recount.

When the phrase "do not fold, bend, spindle, or mutilate" was making the rounds of 1950s American social discourse, a spirited protest emerged, as evidenced through such slogans as "I am a human being; please do not fold, bend, spindle, or mutilate me." Some people were threatened by punch cards and felt that they reduced a human being to nothing more than a card with punched holes, which seemed insulting. In particular, the beatniks of the 1950s—those jazzy, cannabis-loving, bearded, beaten-down beings of beatitude—thought they were more than just a sum of "data."

And they were on to something. In the 1950s, there was a lot of worry about how collectivist, risk-averse, and suburban the American character had become, as though we were all contented to throw away our unpredictable humanity in favor of convenience. One pop sociologist, William H. Whyte, even wrote a book lamenting this trend called *The Organization Man*. The IBM card seemed to embody this conformity, as did all the cookie-cutter suburban houses and the growing network of boring interstate highways. Yet Americans were starting to face an unnerving fact, which is that a great deal of information, from hair color to personality type to crime records, could be entered as *data*.

Punch cards go even further back. Primitive punch cards were invented in 1725, when Basile Bouchon first employed them for textile patterns in France. By the late nineteenth century, punch cards made the player piano possible. In the United States, machine-readable punch cards were prominently used during the 1890 census, when census takers were asked to use their pencils to punch holes in cards instead of writing down their information. Herman Hollerith's census cards had twenty-two rows across and eight columns down, for a total of 176 holes in all. Thus row one, column one might signify male, while row one, column two could signify female. Thomas Watson Sr. of IBM then commercialized the process. By 1928, the number of rows had increased to eighty, and when IBM's great competitor, Remington Rand, came along with its own system, the number of rows had gone up to ninety. That's a lot of information.

By the 1930s, employees were trained and specialized in data entry. They typed the information using a smart new keyboard machine, which then spit out the cards. This allowed governments and corporations to collect data and maintain records more efficiently with each passing year. There were different ways of "programming" cards—such as Fortran, which is a general purpose programming language—and these became the basis for programming computers. Machine-readable punch cards became an enormous and lucrative industry that stretched across North America, Europe, Australia, and even Germany's Third Reich by the 1930s. It serviced the information needs of millions.

Today, thanks to advances in cyber communication and silicon parts, we look at computer screens to analyze data. Six or seven decades ago, it was a manual process of reading cards, then finding the patterns and making the tabulations that computer algorithms perform today. How many dessert forks did Macy's sell last year as opposed to this year? Did it sell more in October or July? Did the price affect the sales? Or might it have been the display—or the brand? Information is power, and everyone from Macy's to the FBI agreed. Thus the fledgling new age of information was launched.

THAT WAS THEN, THIS IS NOW: Punch cards were information. If information in that highly standardized form seemed reductive and dehumanizing to an earlier generation of young people, such as hipsters and beatniks on the verge of the rebellious '60s, for today's young people, information seems liberating. In the form of the World Wide Web, it gives them an endless trove of facts and amusements, interactions and products, images and songs.

HYPOTHETICAL USAGE IN A SENTENCE BY THE OLD AND SETTLED: "Don't fold, bend, spindle, or mutilate that birthday card. It holds a check for forty-nine dollars!" —Ted Emmons, explaining to his family that the latest insulting greeting card from dreaded Great-Aunt Martha shouldn't be automatically torn up—*this* time!

DUM-DEE-DUM-DUM

JUST THE FACTS

#24

TIMELINE: *Dragnet* was a radio and television program that aired on and off from 1949 until the 2000s, but its real TV heyday lasted from 1952 to 1959 and from 1967 to 1970.

INSPIRED GUESS BY TODAY'S YOUNG AND RESTLESS: Tweedledum's younger brother.

THE ANCIENT TRUTH: "Dum-dee-dum-dum" was the opening musical phrase for the most famous cop show that's ever been on television: *Dragnet*. A dragnet is a coordinated police search for the solution of a crime. The popular program *Dragnet* featured two cops: Sergeant Joe Friday and Officer Frank Smith (in the first TV series running from 1951 to 1959) and Sergeant Joe Friday and Officer Bill Gannon (in the second one lasting from 1967 to 1970). The show was a radio favorite starting in the late 1940s, although its true greatness occurred on TV, created and produced by Jack Webb. It lived in syndication for many years, came back to TV in the late 1980s, and returned again in an entirely new format in 2003 (which bombed and was soon canceled). During its heyday, there was a *Dragnet* comic strip and three feature-length *Dragnet* movies. In 1987 Dan Aykroyd and Tom Hanks did a parody film based on *Dragnet*. Now, however, a new generation hath grown up that knows not "dum-dee-dum-dum."

The *Dragnet* theme was composed of the most famous four notes in history, excepting the first four of Beethoven's Symphony no. 5. Earnest and menacing at once, these four notes introduced every episode. Its staccato rhythm was of a piece with the laconic, quick-fire dialogue and set an aesthetic rhythm every week. An announcer would intone that "the story you are about to see [or *hear* if on the radio] is true; the names have been changed to protect the innocent." Soon the voice of Sergeant Joe Friday would take over with his standard opening: "This is the city of Los Angeles, California. I work here. I'm a cop." Viewers would be off on the docudrama of that particular night's episode.

The opening line—"the names have been changed to protect the innocent"—helped create the illusion that the show was a recounting of an otherwise true story. "All we want are the facts, ma'am," said Friday famously. Indeed, the program was a studiously realistic police procedural that held, always, to the most understated documentary style. There was rarely any prolonged violence (sometimes fisticuffs but almost never gunfire). Still, there was an unmistakable whiff of danger and dread.

The array of crimes on *Dragnet* was varied: anything from the murder of a rich man to a hit-and-run to the return of a lost kid to teens hooked on drugs. The point was to show how cops did their work in an authentic way. On the radio version, Webb used genuine sound effects, like the sound of real telephones ringing in the Los Angeles police department. On the radio, when blood was being taken in a backyard, you could hear the vials clinking together and a dog barking faintly in the distance. The show never lapsed into melodrama, for that would be an insult to real-life police officers, whose jobs are routine most of the time. But the show depicted cops who do rough jobs in humdrum circumstances, as well as all the downtime and dead ends that police must endure. In many respects, the greatest struggle *Dragnet* showed was how police officers often had to put their souls on the line and keep their humanity from going out with the tide of weekday filth. Whenever Friday's partners talked cheerfully about their hobbies and fad diets, they were demonstrating that the mean streets had not yet taken away their hearts. Many of the villains on *Dragnet* were banal rather than evil figures, but the depictions of Friday, Smith, and Gannon always demonstrate the small, realistic braveries every day in the lives of ordinary people.

At the end of each episode, the announcer wrapped up by informing viewers about the results of the alleged criminal's trial and sentence, further emphasizing the realistic sense of the show. The program always concluded with the "dum-dee-dum-dum" march.

THAT WAS THEN, THIS IS NOW: Today's millennials would recognize the terse cops featured on *Dragnet*; they've also met them in shows they love, such as *The Wire* and *CSI*. But the old days of gumshoe investigations have been replaced by advanced forensic and DNA testing. Contemporary American police officers and detectives are highly technocratic and often college educated. Sergeant Joe Friday rarely ever sent anything "to the lab." If he were around today, he'd probably be spending more time searching through large databases and less time having laconic conversations with eccentric witnesses and sketchy suspects.

HYPOTHETICAL USAGE IN A SENTENCE BY THE OLD AND SETTLED:

"Dum-dee-dum-dum!" —A teenager in 1958, as he observed his father arriving home late (again) from the bar, enthusiastically anticipating his angry mother's reaction

EDSEL

A CAUTIONARY TALE

TIMELINE: The Ford Edsel was an American automobile manufactured during the 1958, 1959, and 1960 model years.

INSPIRED GUESS BY TODAY'S YOUNG AND RESTLESS: One of the first furry robot toys—some cute little combination of squirrel and bear that squeaked and growled at the same time.

THE ANCIENT TRUTH: Edsel Ford was the son of famous automaker Henry Ford, but he is less well-known as the heir to the Ford Motor Company than for the failed automobile that bore his name (fourteen years after his death). After only three years of production—during which the unsightly vehicle was compared to a toilet seat, a horseshoe, and even an "Oldsmobile sucking a lemon"—the Edsel became an infamous case study of how *not* to make or market a product.

Edsel Ford died in 1943 at age forty-nine, four years before his father did. Tour guides at his historic home in Grosse Pointe Shores, Michigan, now say that Edsel Ford died of an undulant fever caused by the unpasteurized milk his father insisted he drink, even as Edsel hit middle age. The elder Ford, who evidently knew Louis Chevrolet better than he understood Louis Pasteur, thought such a dangerous dairy product was good for the boy.

The car was unveiled in 1957 as the greatest new automotive product since the Model T. Marketers claimed it had "more YOU ideas" than any other car ever made and that it opened a new vista entirely in the experience of driving. There were great reasons to believe the Edsel would succeed. The America of the 1950s was the ultimate car culture. It was a seller's market, and the big carmakers (Ford, General Motors, and Chrysler) were unable to turn out enough cars to meet the demand. By the end of the decade, 80 percent of Americans owned at least one car, and Americans owned more cars than the rest of the world put together. The new network of freeways championed by President Dwight D. Eisenhower, the Interstate Highway System, was in full upswing, which created not only exit ramps, but also drive-in movie theaters, motels, shopping malls, and, of course, McDonald's golden arches. According to the U.S. Census Bureau in 1960, eleven of the twelve largest American cities decreased in population as Americans, equipped with their personal vehicles, headed for the suburbs. Why not introduce another car brand into this lucrative market?

But the Edsel's timing was wrong. With Americans driving farther more often, they began to think a bit more about gas economy. A recession also landed in 1958, and hit hardest were the typical middle-range car models like the Edsel—which was over sixteen feet long. Size and swagger no longer trumped durability, safety, and efficiency. As a result, big, gas-guzzling Packard began desperately to downsize. American Motors moved in the direction of the more fuel-efficient Rambler (which could sleep two in the car, thereby avoiding the expense of motels). By 1960, the small Ford Falcons burst onto the scene, and even Volkswagen Beetles began selling as popular vehicles that would pass many a gas pump before having to succumb to one.

While other mid-range carmakers saw their sales decline in the late 1950s, many of them, such as Buick and Dodge, had built up followings over the years. The Edsel had no such brand loyalty, so it was the first car of its class to be rejected. About 84,000 of them were sold during its three-year run, but this was under half of what Ford needed just to break even. By 1965, the market for middle-range cars—those between a basic Chevy and a luxury Cadillac—had come back. But by then it was too late, and "Edsel" became a synonym for "big bust."

The failure of the Edsel has achieved a certain grim grandeur over the years. Observers look upon the fiasco retrospectively and find all sorts of reasons for the Edsel's demise, but even critics of the time had a field day. They were positive the Edsel had failed because of its poor overall design and gimmicky devices—such as push-button gear shifts on the steering wheel, confusingly near the horn button. But many of those features were ahead of their time—not only the push-button gears, but also the self-adjusting brakes. The Edsel was the right car for the wrong time.

There may have been one other element that led to the Edsel's demise. Its place in the pantheon of Ford was never clear. The genius of General Motors in its heyday was that it made several cars, each of which had its own personality: the unpretentious Chevy, the sporty Pontiac, the confidently powerful Oldsmobile, the solidly upper bourgeois Buick, and the plush Cadillac. It even had clarification within the brands, as the Buick, for instance, had a Special, a Century, a Super, and a Roadmaster, each one slightly more expensive than the previous one. The poor Edsel had an identity crisis. No one seemed sure whether it was a slightly superior Ford or somewhat inferior Mercury, or both, or neither. Sometimes, whether you are a person or an automobile, it is a good idea to understand who you are and what you have to offer—and position yourself accordingly.

THAT WAS THEN, THIS IS NOW: No carmaker would dare create such a hunky-junky, gas-guzzling automobile today. Gas is too costly, and fuel standards are too high—even today's big SUVs get good mileage compared to the old Edsel. A more interesting question would be to ask what young Americans of today think of corporate failures such as Enron and Lehman Brothers. They might find the story of the Edsel to be an amusing blip in what was otherwise a prosperous time. But the collapse of Enron and Lehman Brothers is perhaps a failure that is more keenly felt: it was stuff that threatened the financial stability of the entire world.

HYPOTHETICAL USAGE IN A SENTENCE BY THE OLD AND SETTLED: "I married a Lincoln Continental and had an Edsel within a year." —A young woman in 1962 speaking of her unwise marriage choice; in time, she remarried and is still driving a Dodge, though it's been refurbished twice

"EFFETE CORPS OF IMPUDENT SNOBS"

#26

NIXON'S
NIXON

TIMELINE: This memorable phrase came from Vice President Spiro Agnew in 1969.

INSPIRED GUESS BY TODAY'S YOUNG AND RESTLESS: A grunge rock band.

THE ANCIENT TRUTH: Vice President Spiro T. Agnew first used this phrase to impugn critics of President Richard Nixon's Vietnam policy. The memorable sentence, directed against antiwar protesters, reads as follows: "A spirit of national masochism prevails, encouraged by an effete corps of impudent snobs who characterize themselves as intellectuals." Although "effete corps of impudent snobs" has never quite joined the American political lexicon as a classic, it became famous during the early 1970s as an illustration of how the rhetoric about the war in Vietnam had become inflamed.

Ted Agnew, as his many friends called him, seemed at first to be a fairly clever choice to run with Richard Nixon in 1968. He had been a moderate Republican governor of Maryland, elected on a platform of fair housing laws and antipollution measures. Nixon thought him a proven Democratic vote getter: the governor of a quasi-Southern state, yet not so conservative that he would turn off more liberal Northerners. But once he and Agnew were elected in 1968, Nixon determined that pulling the nation out of the Vietnam War precipitously would risk the appearance of dangerous national weakness. So he decided to stay the course while gradually reducing forces. This put him at immediate odds with a potent antiwar crowd that included liberal Democratic senators and even Walter Cronkite, the respected news anchor, who had said two years before that the war could not be won and that withdrawal was the only prudent and honorable course. Nixon was determined to discredit these critics; Agnew was his chosen weapon.

Fifteen years earlier, President Eisenhower had used Vice President Nixon to make below-the-belt political speeches so Eisenhower could keep his dignity. Now Agnew did the same for President Nixon, thus causing Agnew to be dubbed "Nixon's Nixon" by one wry senator, Eugene McCarthy of Minnesota.

Agnew's speechwriters had a puckish wit and sent him into the arena with truculent charges that antiwar opponents were elitist, snobbish, cowardly, and unmanly. Due to the common perception that America was supposed to be brave, egalitarian, and masculine, critics of the Vietnam War quickly became tagged with the implication that they were either not real Americans or just downright anti-American. The result was to put Nixon's foes over the war on the hind foot. The "silent majority"—or the corps of Americans who were manly and populist and patriotic—rallied to Nixon's side rather than see America lose a war. Agnew's lyrical assonances and consonances didn't hurt the cause.

By early 1973, Nixon had finally found terms for ending the conflict. By then, Agnew's role as pit bull in chief had ended. Despite Nixon's reservations about Agnew's competence, he was on the ticket again in 1972 and remained popular, as are Sarah Palin and Rush Limbaugh today with the most zealous of conservative Republicans. But he assumed a lower profile until 1974, when his past bit him in the form of bribery and extortion charges dating from his days in Maryland politics. He pleaded no contest to one charge, resigned as vice president, and was force-marched into the realm of the forgotten. Sometimes called one of the least prepared vice presidents in history, he became, to emulate one of his own speeches, a self-obliterating orb of obscurity.

THAT WAS THEN, THIS IS NOW: Agnew's invective came out of a particular time—when the nation was irrevocably split between older, patriotic Americans who thought America should never lose a war and younger Americans who believed the intervention in Vietnam was an immoral mistake that needed to end immediately. Many young people thought the recent war in Iraq was likewise an immoral superpower incursion into a foreign land, but there was one big difference: with an all-volunteer army in Iraq, most young men in 2003 had no physical skin in the game and those who did had already signed up in advance.

Had there been a draft to stock soldiers bound for Iraq, a nation that had never attacked the United States, the protest would have been much more incendiary.

HYPOTHETICAL USAGE IN A SENTENCE BY THE OLD AND SETTLED:

"That pink Jaguar in their driveway makes me think the Woosters are an effete corps of impudent snobs." —Mrs. Waddington referring to her neighbors in 1971

EIGHT-TRACK

#27

A BRIEF REVOLUTION IN LISTENING

TIMELINE: Eight-track tape cartridges were popular from about 1965 to 1985.

INSPIRED GUESS BY TODAY'S YOUNG AND RESTLESS: A designer drug of choice.

THE ANCIENT TRUTH: An eight-track is the popular name for an electromagnetic tape with eight "tracks" of music on it *or* the name for the tape player itself. Millions once referred to either or both as an eight-track. Edward Lear, of Learjet fame, is given credit for this invention. An eight-track tape was equivalent to a long-play record (LP) in terms of the length of music it played or (in today's terms) equal to the compact discs you can purchase at what are still called "record" stores. But the eight-track is far more important than simply a bridge between vinyl records and CDs. It was a seminal development in the history of automobile audio, even if its reign lasted only a couple of decades.

The first milestone occurred in 1930, when brothers Paul and Joseph Galvin managed to concoct a radio that ran off the car's electrical system. The radios could be installed as part of the vehicle's equipment—and the telecommunications company Motorola was born. It took thirty years for the radio to become standard equipment on vehicles. Some drivers didn't want the new feature, while others might have liked it but didn't want to pay extra. Nonetheless, a car door had been opened, and once the radio strolled in, it stayed.

The eight-track supplied a listening alternative to the car radio. But earlier, the radio was a great boon for those who wanted to relieve the boredom of just driving along, especially if drivers were by themselves. The problem was that it was a rather inadequate convenience. You had to listen to the music the radio station selected, not the music you would have chosen (as you could with phonographs). No wonder, then, that Chrysler briefly tried car phonographs, but the whole apparatus was too big, and there was no place for it in the interior of the vehicle. A passenger would have been required to regulate it, as changing records while steering an eight-cylinder Buick is exceedingly difficult. Car phonographs were soon off the table—or dashboard.

Yet the answer to this dilemma between phonographs and radio lurked in the technology of tape recordings, *except* that tape recorders were heavy, the reels were large (and hard to load), and the audio quality was poor. Tape recorders worked well for voice but not for music, so the tape recorder somehow had to be reduced in size and the recording fidelity enhanced if it were ever to find an honored place in automobiles.

Above all, as with records, electromagnetic tapes had to be fitted to "tracks" of music, with each track corresponding to the three-minute songs typical of popular music so listeners could do with tapes what they could do with records: listen to all the songs or just the ones that fit their whims. Every seller of recorded music knew that consumers would buy an entire album just to hear two or three favorite songs. A compact, vivid-sounding tape player able to handle eight-tracks would give householders access to music without the clumsy records and phonographs; above all, it would give drivers the music they wanted without having to listen to the radio and hoping against hope that their favorite Patti Page or Perry Como song somehow came along for the ride. The eight-track would liberate Americans from the tyranny imposed by the car radio. Car companies like Ford moved quickly to sponsor research and development into the technology.

All this was easier said than done. Despite interest in eight-track technology, progress was slow. There were drawbacks. Sound hissed and fluttered. Spools wore down easily. The tape itself twisted or wrinkled easily. The disadvantage of tape is the number of moving parts, something largely avoided with the radio. Even when tapes with music got better in terms of physical durability and sound quality, it was still hard, without trial and error, to adjust the length of the tape to the "tracks" of music. Thus some taped music had long silences or extra tunes or other bothersome features that revealed the misfit between tape and tracks. And then it was devilishly hard to skip over one song to find the one you really wanted to hear.

But by 1960, there emerged serviceable eight-track tape players and tapes for them to play. These could be set into the dashboard of the car, and consumer choice reigned. By the mid-1960s, it was indeed a reliable and advanced technology. The quality of sound was high; the durability of the product was consistent. Within ten years, tape players had become a standard feature in autos.

THAT WAS THEN, THIS IS NOW: For today's young people, freedom from the radio is complete. Many of them don't even own a personal radio and prefer listening to music via their laptops and mobile devices instead. In the automobile itself, they have CDs, iPods, and satellite radio that plays over the car's speaker system. Some might say there is no need for a car radio at all unless you want to listen to the news. We might even wonder how much longer the car radio will be a feature in new cars. If car radio goes away—though this is doubtful since many drivers *do* want to listen to talk radio—then by 2030, we may revert to a car-radioless world, such as that of a century before. The more things change, the more they stay the same.

HYPOTHETICAL USAGE IN A SENTENCE BY THE OLD AND SETTLED: "You may have an eight-track tape, but you have a one-track mind." —Mrs. Deborah Kovacs, speaking in 1973 (context best left unknown)

EMILY POST

AMERICA'S
FIRST
MISS MANNERS

TIMELINE: Emily Post enjoyed a successful forty-year career; she was most famous and influential between 1922 and 1946.

INSPIRED GUESS BY THE YOUNG AND RESTLESS: A website like Craigslist that supports female political candidates.

THE ANCIENT TRUTH: Emily Post was a go-to resource for proper manners and social etiquette in American life for a quarter of a century. At her high point, "Emily Post" and "manners" were almost synonymous. In 1922, she wrote a bestselling book, *Etiquette in Society, Business, Politics, and Home*, a comprehensive guide to proper modes of behavior in American life. Her name, seemingly that of a well-starched and propitious New England lady, lives on through the Emily Post Institute, which she founded in 1946.

Emily Post was from Baltimore. An already-established writer, her interest in good manners might have come from the outré behavior of her New York husband, and after her divorce, she discovered that etiquette writing paid off. There was hunger for news of such standards in an upwardly mobile United States, and her accessible, detailed approach attracted a wide audience. Emily Post did not subscribe to the alarmist view that young Americans were necessarily heralds of some new barbarism. Rather, she believed that America's interest in "good taste" was stronger than ever, and young people simply had a different idea of what constituted "good taste." She didn't expect good manners to be followed like a slavish formula. She thought they arose from being raised a certain way—and from a universal common sense and "consideration for the feelings of others." If pressed, she might have admitted that the subject was complex—after all, what is "charming" to one group may not be charming to another. But she clung as much as possible to the idea that her advice was based on pervasive norms.

For Post, manners were ethics. For some people, etiquette was a way of life from birth; for others, it was a matter of learning manners later in life. Above all, she believed that social status did not dictate manners, because anyone could learn them. She was careful to say that the "best" society is not always the most moneyed society. She offered specific advice—almost like medical prescriptions—about acceptable behavior and how to interact with people in a wide range of social situations, including:

- *that women should dress neither too quietly or too trendily but find a personal expression in their garb*
- *that it was both proper and courteous for a man to remove his hat and douse his cigar while talking with ladies*

- *that a house should be stocked with charming items rather than bric-a-brac of purely sentimental value*

Without doubt, Emily Post and her column helped thousands of readers navigate the minefields of tricky social situations.

THAT WAS THEN, THIS IS NOW: Advice on etiquette is not dead. The Emily Post Institute writes columns for such publications as *Good Housekeeping* and *USA Today*, while it also gives seminars on manners to a variety of different organizations. Judith Martin (who refers to herself in the third person as "Miss Manners") has a syndicated *Washington Post* column that offers droll advice about modern etiquette but lacks the more imperious authority of Miss Post. People still want to know how to behave, especially to make a good impression.

However, the world has changed since Emily's counsel was first dispensed, as has the way in which Americans want to move up the social scale. There is a lot of grim talk about how limited American social mobility is these days, but the wish for it remains. Moving to a higher class nowadays means acquiring a boat, a Lexus, a sauna, or even a McMansion. In an earlier time, it was about improving one's demeanor (such as impressing the boss). It was less about material things and more about being (or appearing to be) a certain way. It was about putting on airs (as the prickly critics once put it), not about putting a costly new wing on the house.

HYPOTHETICAL USAGE IN A SENTENCE BY THE OLD AND SETTLED: "Who do you think you are, Emily Post?" —Ruben Schofield in 1929, speaking to his wife after she upbraided him for wearing light brown shoes to a funeral

EXTREMISM IN THE DEFENSE OF LIBERTY

LOOSE LIPS

TIMELINE: Senator Barry Goldwater of Arizona made his memorable—and damaging—remark in the summer of 1964.

INSPIRED GUESS BY TODAY'S YOUNG AND RESTLESS: Sounds like something George Washington or Ted Cruz would say.

THE ANCIENT TRUTH: These are the first six words in one of the most memorable—and politically suicidal—statements in American history: "And let me remind you that extremism in the defense of liberty is no vice, and moderation in the pursuit of freedom is no virtue." Thus Goldwater responded to charges that he was an "extremist" for wanting to end social security and use tactical nuclear weapons to free Eastern Europe from Soviet domination (heedless of prospects for World War III). In doing so, he almost admitted that he *was* an extremist—and proud of it—and thereby helped himself to a big loss. His was an alarmingly eloquent statement of the Republican conservative creed: that some things, especially freedom from big government at home (such as the dependency bred by welfare and the stifling regulations of bureaucrats), along with Soviet tyranny abroad, require *properly* extremist responses. These responses are "no vice."

In this famous statement about extremism, Senator Goldwater had also struck a resounding chord about the peculiar nature of *American* conservatism. A traditional conservative often insists upon the priority of tradition over initiative, of established community norms over radical individualism, of community standards over unfettered liberty. But American conservatism, especially since Goldwater, has taken a different and paradoxical turn. It insists upon the value of *individuality*, and in the history of conservatism, this is a contradiction. This new American conservatism posits a golden, past America: of Minutemen fighting against the cowardly British tyrants who wanted to take their guns away, of solitary cowboys fighting blizzards alone on the lone prairie, and of unconventional entrepreneurs having bright ideas about steel and oil and being unfettered by government regulations.

Goldwater was saying that he and his followers were conservative because they wished to return to unfettered and heroic individual freedom, even if such freedom might be at odds with another conservative goal: the maintenance of tradition and continuity. In effect, this means "Give the entrepreneur the freedom to achieve great things, even if in doing so, he disrupts traditional norms." This is why the same conservatives who champion government restrictions on abortion (they believe in traditional morality) hate government infringement of economic liberty (they believe in unchained liberty). Behind Goldwater's words about extremism and freedom lay a still-unresolved inconsistency.

Yet in the end, Goldwater's viewpoint, however contradictory, won, for just as defeated Confederates in the Civil War used to dream "Save your Confederate money; the South will rise again," so might defeated right-wing Republicans have said, "Don't throw away your goldwater; it will be good to drink someday." And so it was. Americans—weary of Democratic rule in the 1960s and '70s that had been accompanied by race riots, a lost war in Southeast Asia, economic stagnation, and the Iran hostage crisis—finally turned to Goldwater Republicans…two decades later, when Ronald Reagan became president of the United States in 1981. "Extremism" became mainstream. If Goldwater had been a churlish man in horn-rimmed glasses, hearkening back to the covered wagon, Reagan was a charming, affable guy who made conservatism seem modern, even futuristic. Reagan cut taxes (though not as much as he'd have liked), was an unapologetic Cold Warrior (though he carefully stayed out of big wars we couldn't win quickly), and tried to turn welfare into "workfare," all the while maintaining a sunny cheerfulness. He was asked if he was worried by the burgeoning federal deficit. "No, I'm not. It seems to be doing very well on its own!" How can you dislike a swell, good-humored man like that?

THAT WAS THEN, THIS IS NOW: Goldwater spoke to a nation in 1964 that was prosperous. The need for a large federal government, prompted by the Depression and World War II, was slowly being forgotten. But now, nearly fifty years later, the economy is stuck again, and Generation Y knows it. Today's millennials would not share Senator Goldwater's sense of oppression from a vast and paternalistic federal government. Given the high costs of college and the challenging job market (a hangover from the Great Recession), they would like for government to do more, not less. This would include more federal aid toward college education and lower interest rates. They would likely prefer cooperation between the government and the corporate world, which might lead to much-needed job creation. And they wish the government had set down rules that would have prevented the great financial markets crash of 2008.

HYPOTHETICAL USAGE IN A SENTENCE BY THE OLD AND SETTLED:

"Moderation in the pursuit of freedom is no virtue." —Cousin Myrtle speaking to Cousin Elmer (around 1965), defending her freedom to eat a whole box of chocolates before he got even one nugget; because Cousin Elmer was a Goldwater fan, he was quite nonplussed

#30 FATTY ARBUCKLE

HOLLYWOOD'S FIRST GREAT SCANDAL

TIMELINE: Roscoe "Fatty" Arbuckle was a popular silent film actor and entertainer in the 1920s.

INSPIRED GUESS BY TODAY'S YOUNG AND RESTLESS: Politically incorrect description of belt buckle designed for "big and tall" men.

THE ANCIENT TRUTH: Roscoe "Fatty" Arbuckle was a heavy-set man who could dance as lightly as Fred Astaire and do backflips with alacrity. Yet despite his success as an actor, comedian, director, and screenwriter, he is best known for his involvement in Hollywood's first great sex scandal, back when illicit sex was far more shocking to public sensibilities than it is today. Once upon a time, to say the words "Fatty Arbuckle" was to recall a torrid scandal, just as the words "O. J. Simpson" now recall a homicidal sensation. Today we can read racy allegations in nearly every tabloid in nearly every grocery line. The early 1920s was a less jaded time in American life. Even so, the charges against Arbuckle would have caused a stir in our time too.

In 1921, Arbuckle was accused by California authorities of raping and murdering a Hollywood bit player named Virginia Rappe in a hotel. Rappe was a victim of alcohol abuse and was likely poisoned by the poor quality of booze in those days (thank you, Prohibition). As she died she is said to have muttered, "Arbuckle hurt me." This, along with the accusations of a notorious San Francisco madam, was enough to get Fatty indicted for manslaughter. He was tried three times (with a hung jury in the first two trials), and the third time, he was formally acquitted with a profuse apology from the jury.

For over a year during the Arbuckle scandal, lurid headlines kept Americans in a frenzy. ("Arbuckle Faces Gallows," said one newspaper, while another reported, "Fatty Freed in Six Minutes.") It was a good time to invest in the newspaper business, but a terrible time to be Fatty Arbuckle.

The imbroglio ruined Fatty's acting career, as he was unable to find work for the rest of the decade. In the early '30s, a then-alcohol-soaked Arbuckle finally got back into movies (under a pseudonym) as a director. He was even signed by Warner Brothers to do a feature-length film, but that very day in 1933, he died of a heart attack. However, his legacy lives on. After the Arbuckle scandal, Hollywood took steps to shield their stars from salacious publicity—an effort that by no means worked unerringly. The film industry also established an office to regulate the decency of the movies, the Motion Picture Association of America, in 1922. The MPAA was first headed by Will Hays, a former postmaster general of boundless rectitude.

THAT WAS THEN, THIS IS NOW: Arbuckle would be called by his given name Roscoe if he were around today, rather than the politically unfashionable and cruel nickname "Fatty." It's also possible that, if he were found innocent of a crime today, he might have been forgiven by the public much sooner. For whatever reason, we are a society much more prone to giving transgressors second chances (think Richard Nixon). Maybe that's because the concept of "sin" has lost its resonance in contemporary American culture, or maybe it's because we forget about past peccadilloes much faster now—since the subject changes so much more rapidly in this time of information overload.

HYPOTHETICAL USAGE IN A SENTENCE BY THE OLD AND SETTLED: "I'm as innocent as Fatty Arbuckle—and much thinner too." —Someone's great-grandfather after his wife accused him of infidelity with the church organist in 1940

FLUB-A-DUB

DARWINIAN
POTPOURRI OF
DOODYVILLE

TIMELINE: *The Howdy Doody Show*, which featured Flub-a-Dub and his hometown of Doodyville, ran on NBC from 1947 to 1960.

INSPIRED GUESS BY TODAY'S YOUNG AND RESTLESS: A word that must indicate all the *flubs* (boneheaded mistakes) of George "Dubya" Bush.

THE ANCIENT TRUTH: Flub-a-Dub was a fabulous puppet on the once-famed kids' TV program *The Howdy Doody Show*. Flub-a-Dub was a creature composed of eight different animals: duck, cat, giraffe, cocker spaniel, seal, raccoon, and dachshund. If the kids who watched *Howdy Doody* grew up to be Deadheads, they started out as Doodyheads. Flub was part of what invaded their little noggins from 5:30 to 6:00 Eastern every weekday afternoon.

Flub was part of the show's circus tradition. He was a kind of timorous and reassuring sideshow freak (see **Bearded Lady**), the sort who wouldn't frighten children. Another *Howdy Doody* character in the same tradition was Clarabell the Clown. He communicated entirely with bike horn and seltzer bottle, honking the horn to register enthusiasm and squirting the bottle at someone to express displeasure. (His emotional repartee was limited and primitive until the last show in 1960, when he had a tear in his painted eye and whispered good-bye to the kids.)

The actor who first played Clarabell was Bob Keeshan, who went on to star as Captain Kangaroo, but the gentle future Captain left the role of Clarabell in 1952 after a very adult-like spat over salary.

Howdy Doody was a sort of Huck Finn–looking American type: he had red hair and forty-eight freckles, one for each of the states back then. He wore a red bandanna, checked Western shirt, and blue jeans and spoke in an "aw shucks" kid's voice that sounded suspiciously like that of his pal, Buffalo Bob Smith, the show's adult host. Bob presided over all this silliness and dressed in buckskin, a nod to not one but two great American images: the circus and the Western frontier.

Any real-life unpleasantness was kept from the kids, such as when Bob Smith had a heart attack and was said to be "vacationing at Pioneer Village" for six weeks (while he was in fact recovering). But in 1971, public affairs commentator Jeff Greenfield argued that the show had antiestablishment undertones and that the young viewers were probably aware of it on some level. Greenfield said that Clarabell, with his manic water bottle that he wielded like a weapon, was the nation's first hippie, full of absurdist rebellion for which that 60s youth type became famous. In fact, Clarabell might have been the first countercultural role model these youngsters ever encountered. It should surely be added that even the character of Mayor Bluster had a corrupt side. Was a latent cynicism implanted along with all the innocent merriment? After all, these same kids grew up to organize street theater protests against the establishment in such places as San Francisco and New York!

These tongue-in-cheek arguments are fun, but *The Howdy Doody Show* was mostly a kid-sitting enterprise, and as such it had all the salient features that "the tube" is supposed to provide young viewers (and their weary parents). It offered the reassurance of familiar motifs—the circus and the Western. It presented a goofy but familiar world—anyone who has raised little kids knows that they paradoxically cling to both the regular and the ridiculous at once. Doodyville was populated by eager kids, amazing creatures, a chaotic clown, a Native American chief (Thunderthud), and a princess (Summerfallwinterspring), America's "number-one detective" (John J. Fadoozle), and Mayor Bluster's brother, Don Jose Bluster. None of this made sense, yet it all made sense, much like another world to follow in which there were big birds, garbage addicts, cookie monsters, and numerically obsessed counts.

THAT WAS THEN, THIS IS NOW: Doodyville wasn't nearly as educational as *Sesame Street* and *Mister Rogers' Neighborhood* were, but then it was on commercial, not public, television. Besides, Mom tended to be home all the time during the *Howdy Doody* years, ready to help her offspring with their sums and alphabet. After she entered the workforce some twenty years later, as the economy required two household incomes and the divorce rate skyrocketed, the children were lucky to have Bert and Ernie for company, both social and educational.

HYPOTHETICAL USAGE IN A SENTENCE BY THE OLD AND SETTLED:
"Multiple personality disorder might have been called Flub-a-Dub syndrome, but despite my best scholarly efforts, it never was." —Professor E. Van Steven, University of Southern North Dakota, about 1963

FORTY-FIVE (45) RPM

THE RECORD WITH THE DOUGHNUT HOLE

TIMELINE: Forty-five rpm records first appeared in the late 1940s; they were superseded by cassette tapes by the 1980s and by compact discs by the 1990s.

INSPIRED GUESS BY TODAY'S YOUNG AND RESTLESS: The number of rounds that an assault weapon can fire in one minute.

THE ANCIENT TRUTH: Forty-five rpm means "forty-five revolutions per minute," and it refers to the number of times that a seven-inch analog record revolves in sixty seconds. By the mid- to late 1950s, "the 45" record had emerged quickly and aggressively as the preferred format to record and play music. They replaced the 78 rpm gramophone records of the 1920s to 1940s. The lightweight 45 could store more music than its predecessor and fit approximately a single three-minute song per side

(which were known as "A" and "B" sides). When Elvis Presley first began selling records in the early 1950s, generally in the South where advanced technology lagged, most of his songs were on 78s. Just a few years later in 1960, most of his record sales were 45s. As a result of 45s, the "singles" market was created and led to Top 40 pop radio.

Elvis and the old crooner Bing Crosby died within two months of each other in 1977. Bing was seventy-four; Elvis was forty-two. They had both been fabulously popular in their day, but if Crosby was "made" by the 1930s radio, which was ideally suited to pick up his light, casual tones—no opera singer he— then Elvis was "made" by the 1950s portable record player.

The portable record player of the 1950s consisted of plastic records that were played courtesy of a small needle attached to an armature. The needle converted the tiny grooves on the spinning plastic record into recorded sounds, a speaker in the machine enhanced the experience of listening, and voilà—you had Elvis and "Hound Dog" in your bedroom. You swooned. The "bedroom" part is especially important, for 45 rpm records with their bagel-like holes were small and light and could be played on a portable, lightweight record player. You no longer needed to depend on your parents' big phonograph in the living room. You had your own player in your bedroom. Here the separate youth culture with which we are familiar today had its beginnings.

Forty-five rpm records only required a small phonograph to be played. Listeners could also stack together a group of records using a plastic adapter, which would allow the record player to deliver the discs in the order they were placed (similar to how mp3 playlists are created today). Some 45 record players, lacking speakers, could be plugged into the back of a radio jack for added volume. The 45 phonograph was the closest thing to portable music until the rise of the transistor radio of the 1960s and the Walkman of the 1980s. By 1955, the days of having to rely on Mom and Dad's enormous phonograph, of having your record and dance parties under their prying eyes, were over. Young people were free to listen to their own preferred music, essentially wherever and whenever they wanted.

> The world of vinyl seems foreign to music fans today. We showed a current college student a portable 45 rpm record player, and in response, he asked, "How could you jog with it?" *Portable* doesn't mean what it used to.
>
> Imagine shopping for the best "needle" you could afford or wincing (or crying even) when you scratched a favorite record by failing to lift the stylus off carefully enough. Think of how happy you would have been when records became as flexible as to be well-nigh "unbreakable."

THAT WAS THEN, THIS IS NOW: Despite the immense popularity of the 45, technological advances soon led to magnetic tape cassettes in the early 1980s, with improved production values and affordability. Of course, cassettes paved the way for compact discs in the 1990s, and today, mp3 devices and digital streaming on laptops and smartphones (through services such as iTunes and Pandora Internet Radio) are the most popular ways to listen to music.

Today's record sales are a shadow of what they were a quarter century ago. But they are rising again, as more and more young people are discovering the tactile and nostalgic joys of "going vinyl." Digital audio quality, in which every bit of sound is rounded off to the nearest and perfect pitch, will always beat analog. But if you are a person of a certain age, save those antique "Heartbreak Hotels" and other corpses from the olden groove yard. *Antiques Roadshow* and eBay await you.

HYPOTHETICAL USAGE IN A SENTENCE BY THE OLD AND SETTLED:

"Suppose I take these 45s and turn them into picnic plates." —Sylvester Humbert, who had his children late in life, registering his rather low opinion of all those Little Richard tunes his daughters play, over and over and over, around 1956

FRANCIS THE TALKING MULE

#33

THE ARMY'S FAVORITE QUADRUPED

TIMELINE: Francis was a talking mule who starred in seven popular movies in the 1950s.

INSPIRED GUESS BY TODAY'S YOUNG AND RESTLESS: A short-lived character on *Sesame Street*.

THE ANCIENT TRUTH: Francis could talk as well as you and I—as long as he had a voice-over and a trainer pulling nylon thread through his teeth to induce him to move his mouth. It's an ironic story, starting with the fact that Francis was really a female mule—and a very trainable one. No one watching the stupendously popular movies in which Francis appeared could tell the gender difference.

Some observers might argue that the great commercial success of the seven *Francis the Talking Mule* movies were a tribute to the childish and unthinking tastes of the era. The dominant idea is that the '50s were a time of denial, boredom, and repression—with Eisenhower in charge of a feel-good presidency, a forced-march return of American women to the kitchen, and the endless conformity of look-alike split-level suburban homes. If so, then Francis himself was a conformist. Asked in the movies by amazed generals to state his name, rank, and serial number, he would dutifully do so. (He was in the Mule Division of the United States Army.) He wanted nothing but the best for the army, and he had a real penchant for helping out the underdog, who was played in six of the seven films by the dancer and comedian Donald O'Connor. O'Connor's character, Private Stirling, was naive and incompetent, lucky enough to have as an ally an unsuspicious but precocious mule. By being able to overhear secret information gleaned from army brass, who never thought a thing of sealing their lips in the presence of a mule, Francis was able to communicate vital facts to Private Stirling, with whom Francis uniquely spoke in a gravel-like, Western drawl. Perhaps Francis, who was used to being underestimated himself, found common cause with this fellow underrated figure.

Francis and Stirling went places that a private of very average intelligence would otherwise not go without a voluble mule to advance the plot. Thus they embarked on comical adventures to the realms of West Point, big cities, haunted houses, and racetracks. After six of these films, Donald O'Connor finally quit as the human lead in favor of Mickey Rooney because, O'Connor claimed, he received less fan mail than the mule did.

The Francis movies are painfully dated. Yet the whole notion does rest on a common, universal theme: companionship with animals. Young persons today, who would turn their noses skyward (and who could blame them) at a single Francis movie, also have lovable cats, dogs, horses, gerbils, turtles—even pythons. Children talk to their pets and imagine that they can talk back, in their fashion. (Some "older children," now as elderly as ninety, even put words in their mouths.) The fanciful but persistent idea that our domesticated friends can speak to us (in our own tongue, no less) continued into the 1960s too, in a show called *Mr. Ed* (with the same producer as the Francis films). Mr. Ed was a talking horse, yet his was a popular show during an era when young Americans were getting stoned and sleeping around. Even in times of rebellion, there's always room for a talking animal, as the enduring popularity of Jim Davis's 1978 cartoon creation *Garfield*, the lazy cat who hates diet, exercise, and Mondays, surely demonstrates. Given the popularity of such talking "real" (not cartoon) animals as Babe and the two dogs and a cat in *Homeward Bound*, perhaps Francis didn't just reveal army secrets—perhaps he unwittingly paved the way for later generations of chattering quadrupeds.

THAT WAS THEN, THIS IS NOW: A useful comparison resides in the contrast between Francis of the 1950s and today's more contemporary talking donkey: the appropriately named Donkey from the animated series *Shrek*. While Francis had little personality of his own other than to be the droll voice of secret information for the bumbling PFC Stirling, Donkey in *Shrek* is an equine version of a friend you might know, who talks incessantly and irritably but who is nearly always glad—yet gets his feelings hurt with altogether too much facility. Francis was a plot device; Donkey is a social type. Francis was an appealing eavesdropper; Donkey is a likable dork.

HYPOTHETICAL USAGE IN A SENTENCE BY THE OLD AND SETTLED:

"You may think naming our first son Francis is okay because everyone will call him 'Frank,' but isn't it just as likely they'll call him a talking mule?" —Delbert Forbes, thirty, speaking to his wife in 1953

GEORGE "KINGFISH" STEVENS

#34

THE KING OF LARCENY

TIMELINE: George "Kingfish" Stevens was one of three key African American characters on *The Amos 'n' Andy Show*, which ran on the radio from 1928 to 1960, with a TV adaptation on CBS from 1951 to 1953 and in syndication until 1966. Its heyday was the '30s and '40s.

INSPIRED GUESS BY TODAY'S YOUNG AND RESTLESS: An old Tea Party senator from Louisiana.

THE ANCIENT TRUTH: The popular situation comedy *Amos 'n' Andy* was a "do-not-miss" feature of American entertainment for nearly twenty years. The original radio program was the brainchild of two white comedians, Freeman Gosden and Charles Correll. They came up with the names Amos and Andy after hearing two elderly African American men address each other as such in an elevator, and their new program premiered on Chicago's radio station

WMAQ in 1928. The premise of the show followed the two titular characters after they left a farm in Georgia and moved to Chicago to found a taxi company. The naive, industrious Amos (voiced by Gosden) and the dreamy, gullible Andy (played by Correll) made friends with George "the Kingfish" Stevens (again voiced by Gosden), a crafty man who often preyed on Andy's dreams of making a fast buck. But the Kingfish had his own wild fantasies of instant riches, so his schemes generally collapsed into hilarity. The country laughed aloud every weeknight, and the show became an addictive habit for millions. The Kingfish's recurring catchphrase "holy mackerel!" was repeated throughout the nation.

By the mid-1930s, *Amos 'n' Andy* was so popular that movie theaters would stop their films for fifteen minutes so filmgoers could listen to the duration of the program through the movie house's loudspeaker system.

Why was the show so popular? The talented writing and radio acting of Gosden and Correll had a great deal to do with it. They were masters of malapropisms, the comic misuse of vocabulary (such as saying "ultimato" for "ultimatum"). They also created hilarious, hapless plots and knew how to balance the comedy with good-hearted sentimentality. However, many listeners took offense at the idea of white actors playing African Americans, and controversy over the program quickly mounted.

In 1951, *Amos 'n' Andy* transitioned from radio to TV, and for the first time, professional African American actors were cast as the major characters—such as actor Tim Moore, who rocketed to fame with his portrayal of the Kingfish. The show switched its fictional setting from

Chicago to Harlem and became a weekly thirty-minute show (complete with live audience) rather than a nightly fifteen-minute one. Gosden and Correll continued as the presiding geniuses of the TV show and hired excellent screenwriters to assist them. But the days of *Amos 'n' Andy* were numbered.

Almost from the outset of the radio show, civil rights leaders spoke out against the show's problematic depiction of African Americans and collected over 875,000 signatures on a petition. Many people felt the characters were presented as unfair caricatures rather than real people: Andy as stupid, Lightning (the indolent janitor at Amos and Andy's lodge) as lazy, and the Kingfish as a swindler. Their use of bad grammar and mispronunciation in dialogue was also deemed racist, as it suggested that African Americans were uneducated. Once the modern civil rights movement began in the 1960s, pressure from the NAACP intensified. CBS canceled the TV version in 1953, and by 1966, the network withdrew it from all syndication, for by then the country had seen the passage of two landmark civil rights bills. Correll died in the early 1970s, and ten years later, Gosden did too.

THAT WAS THEN, THIS IS NOW: The show is the racist product of an early America. In today's culture, *Amos 'n' Andy* would be a total nonstarter. Yet this is not quite the end of the story, for if *Amos 'n' Andy* is gone, the sitcom is not. In fact, in 1972, fewer than fifteen years after the death of the radio show, there was another popular black sitcom on network TV. This was *Sanford and Son*, set in the Watts area of Los Angeles. It portrayed an endearing, if gruff, main character. Although Fred Sanford had his own issues with prejudice, he was portrayed as a complex human being, and not a simplistic, demeaning African American stereotype. This was progress indeed.

Above all, there is something about the sitcom itself that will always remain popular and relevant, whether it be a mainstream one like *Cheers* or a specialized one like the teen-directed *The OC* or the college-age-directed *Girls*. And what is that enduring sitcom appeal? It's our need to be part of a group, to be able to drop in on weekly friends and enjoy their all-too-predictable qualities and flaws under the pressures of a social life we all recognize and relate to. We all understand the daily problems, often comic, entailed by the need to be loyal, tactful, honest, and tolerant. Indeed, so strong is this appeal that, for millions of Americans, to miss the last episode of *Friends* in 2004 would have seemed an act of disloyalty.

HYPOTHETICAL USAGE IN A SENTENCE BY THE OLD AND SETTLED:

"You must think you're George Kingfish Stevens and I'm Andy Brown." —Wilbur Calaboose, speaking in 1938 to his cousin Egbert, after Egbert assured Wilbur that buying property in Vermont "riddled with uranium" was a surefire investment

GOING GARBO

THE FIRST TO GO DARK

#35

TIMELINE: Greta Garbo's golden age as an actress was in the 1930s, and she retired in the late 1940s.

INSPIRED GUESS BY TODAY'S YOUNG AND RESTLESS: Probably a variation of "going gaga" or "going crazy."

THE ANCIENT TRUTH: "Going Garbo" was a phrase that referred to the great 1920s and '30s movie star Greta Garbo, famous for her reticence and refusal of interviews and autographs. "Going Garbo" was therefore used to describe a person's preference for being alone and her fierce sense of privacy. So introverted was Garbo that when she was awarded an honorary Oscar in 1954, the Academy of Motion Pictures had to send it to her home because she refused to attend the ceremony. Many of her most famous movies included her saying "I want to be alone" or similar variations. She once described media glare as a murderer of true love. By

1950, after she had become a recluse in New York City, having retired from the silver screen, she made a distinction that she had plenty of friends and lovers, but she didn't want to be bothered by strangers. Garbo spotting became a sport in Manhattan during the 1930s, but as she got older and the dark glasses larger, it became harder and harder to do.

As a young woman in her native Sweden, she started out as a fashion model and studied acting. Even after Garbo went to Hollywood to pursue her sensational career, three deaths afflicted her significantly: those of her beloved sister and father, and that of Mauritz Stiller, the director who discovered her in Sweden. After an impoverished childhood, trouble followed her in life, and she played, to wildly popular effect, troubled women on the silver screen.

Garbo was able to take all sorts of bad stuff, whether real or scripted, and transmute it into her unique cinematic art. While she was almost supernaturally beautiful, her art was her truest gift: her magical eyes could flash love, longing, jealousy, hatred, resentment, and above all, suffering. She made dying for love look glamorous. Her various roles, including those of vamp, courtesan, spy, prostitute, and queen, often came down to the same pervasive themes: love of which the misaligned stars disapprove and the acrid ironies and injustices of fate. Even in her deathbed scenes (she was especially sexy when reclining), Garbo exuded regal magnificence while facing her own demise.

But even her acting method was all about being alone: she insisted on a closed set so that the exquisite precision of her pretending would not be disturbed. From the time she was a young girl, she possessed a great imagination. She guarded it and kept it to herself, and away from media and fans, as much as she could. This made her a woman of mystery. So famously mysterious was she that her studio, MGM, trumpeted even the most inane things she did as downright revolutionary. When they cast her in a talking movie, the studio shouted, "GARBO TALKS!" or "GARBO LAUGHS!" Her voice, European, husky, and androgynous, was electric: "Get me a whiskey with ginger ale on the side and don't be stingy about it."

THAT WAS THEN, THIS IS NOW: So how would Generation Y react to "the Swedish Sphinx"? They would find her modus operandi unusual. Given the usual mania for celebrity information and exposure today (for example, the popularity of gossip sites like TMZ), it would be much more difficult for Garbo to avoid the spotlight today. Or if she did, for a time, it would just be perceived as an act to prevent overexposure and promote an image. But there is one way in which Garbo and today's millennials align. The expression "going dark" is Gen Y's version of "going Garbo." It means that one has declared that for the next number of hours or days, one is going to be unavailable through email, text messaging, social media, Skype, etc., and taking a break from the endless cycle of "being connected." Garbo once famously said, "I want to be let alone." Gen Y says, on occasion, "I want a break."

HYPOTHETICAL USAGE IN A SENTENCE BY THE OLD AND SETTLED: "I fear Susie is 'going Garbo' this afternoon." —Mrs. Wilcox, describing her ten-year-old daughter's refusal to come out of her tree house, July 1936

GOOD EVENING, MR. AND MRS. AMERICA, AND ALL THE SHIPS AT SEA

AMERICA'S FAVORITE STACCATO

#36

TIMELINE: Walter Winchell's heyday as a radio gossip columnist and newscaster was in the 1930s and '40s.

INSPIRED GUESS BY TODAY'S YOUNG AND RESTLESS: The introduction to an old TV program about a crazy but funny ship captain.

THE ANCIENT TRUTH: Walter Winchell was the most popular and acclaimed newspaper gossip columnist and radio news commentator of the American 1930s and '40s. "Good evening, Mr. and Mrs. America" was how he greeted listeners to his 1940s news program, which was once among the most listened to on the radio dial. Winchell delivered this opening accompanied by a telegraph key, which squealed out staccato rhythms with a potent sense of emergency. Winchell's voice was equally urgent and went on like a tommy gun. (In fact,

Winchell reportedly would not urinate until after each broadcast because he thought the discomfort would speed up his breathless and informative palaver.) For all the speed of his delivery, his enunciation was perfect. He never tripped over words. He would deliver several news items per broadcast, with the sounds of a ticker tape machine between them—no more than a few seconds each. His broadcast was in a newspaper format with datelines, as in "Chicago" or "Manchester, New Hampshire" or "Moscow."

Winchell was born in New York City in 1897 and became a news reporter after a stint in vaudeville. Early on in his career, he developed a voracious appetite for tidbits of information that few parties were supposed to know. Winchell himself often revealed information that *he* had promised to keep quiet about. High-minded journalists thought Winchell was a fungus on their professional standards. In response, he mined the gutter and made himself the story. He used questionable tactics to get information, compromised his journalistic neutrality with personal vendettas, and always preferred the "hot" story to the truly important one.

He was the first great and powerful gossip columnist, appearing in the *New York Daily Mirror* and syndicated all over the country. At the height of his career, celebrities feared him, and even the rich and influential hesitated to tangle with him, although at times throughout his career, he was afraid *he* would be harmed because of the secrets he carried. Winchell took care to ensure his contracts protected him against libel; rather, the newspapers and the radio networks would assume all responsibility. That made him heedless in what he would write and publish.

Winchell was instantly recognizable as the prototypical American urban man. He wore a newsman's serviceable fedora hat, smoked, and wore a dark overcoat. He was really the first *infotainer*. (This is precisely the sort of buzzword that Winchell, who was adept at minting new words, would have loved.) The word didn't exist then, but a typical Winchell broadcast would range from reports on Roosevelt's latest summit meeting with Stalin to a recently divorced celebrity's decision to elope with a starlet. He blended the portentously serious with the gossipy inane—and thus he delivered something for everyone. He would often sign off with pithy advice for world leaders. He would refer to himself humbly as "your reporter," but Mr. and Mrs. America and all the ships at sea knew that he was more than that: he was the insider. He feuded with many and exposed many more, but, it seemed, he would always go on being Winchell: the guy with the real dope, outrageous and brave, indifferent to whose ox he gored, and largely immune from libel.

He used pejorative euphemisms ("infanticipate" for pregnant, "renovated" for divorced, and "mister and miseries" to indicate martial trouble). These "winchellisms" were essential to his technique. They not only kept him out of trouble; they also established his smart wit. Best of all, winchellisms offered a faster, easier way to deliver information. It takes fewer words to say "Charlie Chaplin and wife, mister and miseries" than to say "Charlie Chaplin and his wife are having marital difficulties." And every second counted. Winchell could speak between 197 and 227 words per minute. If you think this is easy to do while also being understandable, give it a try when no one else is at home.

The last fifteen years of his life were ugly. He grew increasingly reckless, especially when he became a fan of the vicious and eventually disgraced Communist-hunter Senator Joe McCarthy. But mostly it was that Winchell could never make it in TV. His rapid-fire, juicy bits of entertainment worked in print and on the radio, but when he sat before cameras with his hat on, he seemed ridiculous: hyper in a relaxed medium, old and ugly as the camera caught every wrinkle. But he wouldn't or couldn't change a thing. He was so rigid that he killed himself off. In his heyday, he might have called it "inflexicide."

THAT WAS THEN, THIS IS NOW: Winchell's machine-gun style would be too heated and outmoded for today's more casual style of reporting. The smooth and relaxed Brian Williams he was not, nor was he the arch, sardonic Jon Stewart. What's more, the Internet has given us more gossip than we can possibly keep up with. If Winchell tried to survive as an "exclusive" source, he wouldn't last a week.

HYPOTHETICAL USAGE IN A SENTENCE BY THE OLD AND SETTLED: "Good evening, Mr. and Mrs. America, and all the ships at sea. Let's go to press. Dateline: our front yard. Old Man Nearing actually said something nice to me today." —Old Man Nearing's next-door neighbor, 1942

#37 HOPALONG CASSIDY

THE TEETOTALING COWBOY

TIMELINE: Hopalong Cassidy was the name of a famous fictional, heroic cowboy brought to life on the big screen by actor William Boyd in the 1930s.

INSPIRED GUESS BY TODAY'S YOUNG AND RESTLESS: A cartoon bunny rabbit from the ancient 1960s.

THE ANCIENT TRUTH: Hopalong Cassidy was first created by author Clarence Mulford in his novels. By the mid-1930s, Hopalong had come to the silver screen. In its heyday, Hopalong was an entire franchise, featuring two or three popular B-Westerns a year, a comic strip, kids' toys ranging from lunch boxes to roller skates, a short-lived theme park called Hoppyland (opened in Venice, California, in 1951 and closed in 1954), and Hoppy's visage on the covers of national magazines. Hopalong was also a big success on both radio and television during the late 1940s and early 1950s.

Hopalong Cassidy was so named thanks to his characteristically jumpy gait, the result of a gunshot to the leg. The character made William Boyd a rich man. Boyd could not ride a bronco or fix a barbed wire fence. In fact, until the Hoppy series came along in 1935, he was, at forty, a declining Hollywood player who had done best in silent films. But in accepting the role of Hoppy, Boyd had latched on to a good thing—and rode it as hard as Hoppy rode his white horse Topper. In fact, when the film series stalled in the mid-1940s, Boyd mortgaged his house to buy the rights and keep it going. It was the best decision he ever made, as the series had a lot of good horse riding ahead of it after all.

> William Boyd took his role very seriously and was keenly aware of his own cultural significance. In his later years, he would not give interviews because he did not want to disillusion those who as youngsters had idolized him as Hopalong Cassidy.

Boyd's Hoppy was a different sort of cowboy star. Unlike Gene Autry and Roy Rogers, he never sang a note. Unlike traditional TV cowboys who wore brighter colors, he wore all black (the popular convention of the time was that only the bad guys wore black). Polite and civilized, he made a point of never drinking alcohol but would self-consciously order either sarsaparilla or even milk at bars. He never started a fight but rather always let the bad guy swing first. He solved the murders of innocent gold miners and ran down rustlers in order to settle range wars. He was accompanied by two companions: a young and impulsive guy named Speedy McGinnis who was a little too quick to fall for—and try to save—the ladies in trouble; and an older geezer, California Carlson, who was equally impulsive but awkward and rude. Speedy or Carlson said whatever they thought, regardless of decorum, and these characters functioned as both comic relief and cautionary tales.

Hoppy's personal cowboy code went something like this: help damsels in distress but be patient and careful about it; say what you think but within limits; be tough but a true gent; ride a white horse; and if you drink milk, as you should, make sure it's purest white. Thus did Hoppy help give impressionable young boys a firm foundation in morality.

THAT WAS THEN, THIS IS NOW: If Gen Y wants to look in on Old Hoppy, there are plenty of DVDs available. There is still an annual Hoppy Day in Boyd's hometown of Cambridge, Ohio; it began in 1991. But today's small fry would find the Hoppy films much too low-tech for them. They have come to expect a fairly dazzling array of special effects thanks to digital animation, so watching Hopalong shoot a rustler wouldn't be much more exciting than watching a man out the window jogging with his cocker spaniel. Hoppy was virtuous and decisive, but for a nine-year-old today, bred on cyber dramas and video games in which they get to become a different person and act out in a different world, Hoppy would be a bore.

HYPOTHETICAL USAGE IN A SENTENCE BY THE OLD AND SETTLED:
"If Hopalong Cassidy had had castor oil back in his day, I'm sure *he'd* have taken it." —Your great-grandmother trying to get your grandfather to take medicine in about 1938

IN LIKE FLYNN

A
SALACIOUS MAN
INDEED

#38

TIMELINE: The origin of the phrase probably dates from 1942, when movie star Errol Flynn sealed his reputation as a womanizer.

INSPIRED GUESS BY TODAY'S YOUNG AND RESTLESS: Must refer to Flynn Rider, the rogue who rescues Rapunzel in Disney's *Tangled*.

THE ANCIENT TRUTH: "In like Flynn," a popular American expression from the 1940s until the 1970s, was almost surely based on the sexual exploits of a Hollywood star of the '30s and '40s named Errol Flynn. To be sure, some in the 1940s denied this allegation and insisted that the expression was based on the political boss of the Bronx, Ed Flynn, since anyone endorsed by Boss Flynn was "in" when it came to elections or appointments. But the popular belief endured. In 1942, Flynn was accused of having sex with underage Hollywood girls. He was acquitted, but the image stuck as a man who got "in" easily. For example, during World War II, when something went well, soldiers would say we're "in like Flynn," which expressed relief at escaping peril. The GIs also meant that the sooner the war was over, they would also be "in like Flynn" by celebrating in various foreign ports or even back home.

Flynn himself was born in Tasmania but claimed to be Irish. In 1926, when he was seventeen, he was kicked out of school for bedding a laundress; but by the early 1930s, when he was in his mid-twenties, he found his way to acting in England and then to Hollywood. By 1935, his athletic sidestepping, especially with dazzling swordplay, made him a star in Hollywood films of "swashbuckling"—named for the noise that a side sword makes when it hits the buckle, or shield, of the opponent. He was a talented actor, but the fact that Flynn was thin and handsome and mustachioed also helped his erotic agenda on the silver screen.

Flynn reportedly designed his house in Hollywood so that he could bug the ladies' bathrooms. He was an addicted voyeur who was declared unfit for military service because of, among other maladies, a heart murmur and venereal disease—and was accused of cowardice by his critics. This was a nightmare for his studio, Warner Brothers, because revealing his poor health would have ruined Flynn's suave image, but not doing so meant that the unpatriotic charge would stick.

It seems that, for Errol, a screwdriver for breakfast and a prostitute for lunch were often on the menu. He married three times and bedded now-unrecalled Hollywood beauties such as Dolores del Río. But despite his troubled reputation, his films remained popular even after the underage sex scandal.

Toward the end of his life, in 1958, he wrote (with a ghostwriter) a highly acclaimed autobiography called *My Wicked, Wicked Ways* (he wanted to call it *In Like Me*, but the publisher wisely declined the notion). In it, he confessed a great many of his sins but managed to justify most of them on the grounds that knowledge (carnal, sensual outer limits) is what man is made for. He wrote that few men have "taken into their maw more of life than I" and that while he had a great rage to live, he had "twice the urge to die." It seems that while he may have been Robin Hood on-screen, off it he was Dorian Gray, Oscar Wilde's character who was obsessed with the subject of aging and how to escape from it. Flynn reported that he hated to be known for his promiscuous reputation but admitted that he had done just about everything he could to cling to fame. Indeed, a national organization called ABCDEF (American Boys Club for the Defense of Errol Flynn) shamelessly supported him throughout his career, until his death in 1959.

THAT WAS THEN, THIS IS NOW: Today no one remembers Errol Flynn and thus has no clue that the phrase "in like Flynn" originally referred to sexual promiscuity. We are now on the other side of the sexual revolution of the 1960s, yet sex outside marriage and other conventional boundaries remain common. Even so, Errol Flynn's reputation would not shock us today the way he shocked an earlier generation. Relatively few have been utterly outraged by even worse charges against director Roman Polanski in 1977. Being "in like Flynn" isn't quite the accomplishment it used to be!

HYPOTHETICAL USAGE IN A SENTENCE BY THE OLD AND SETTLED:

"Ah, the right key at last: we're in like Flynn." —Bobby Gusher, fifteen, speaking to Dwight Dunne, fourteen, in 1948, as they unlocked Bobby's father's liquor cabinet

ISOLATION BOOTH

#39

QUIZ SHOW SWINDLE

TIMELINE: Isolation booths were devices used in prime-time TV quiz shows throughout the "Golden Age of Television" (1948 to 1959).

INSPIRED GUESS BY TODAY'S YOUNG AND RESTLESS: Name of a website that explains detachment techniques in order to aid meditation.

THE ANCIENT TRUTH: Isolation booths were small, enclosed glass structures featured in popular game shows such as *The $64,000 Question* and *Twenty One*. In the isolation booth, contestants were totally cut off from corrupting influences (such as spontaneous help shouted from the audience), and it also prevented players from hearing each other's answers, which made the shows seem "honest." These wildly popular programs captivated the fifty million people watching at home in a period where the television was still a burgeoning medium. (Americans have always loved the solitary hero who does not crack under pressure.) For successful contestants, there was big money and minor celebrity status. For the networks and sponsors of the quiz shows, such as the makers of lipstick and higher energy tonics treating **tired blood**, strong viewership equaled high ratings and huge sales. As a result, the numerous game shows of the period were forced to compete against each other for good ratings. And this led to their becoming more and more show biz and scripted—and in time, they also found the dark road to corruption.

The quiz shows were an intellectual "high tide" for an America in which, briefly, well-educated thinkers were admired by a national audience. Young scholars were encouraged to do their homework so that they too someday might enter an isolation booth, win thousands of dollars, and become known forever after as a world-class expert—such as the marine captain who had an encyclopedic knowledge of cooking, the psychologist who knew everything about boxing, and even an Italian American shoemaker who knew his opera. He not only won $64,000—a king's ransom in 1956 and $550,000 in 2014 terms—but was even invited to the La Scala opera and an audience with the pope. The stakes were high and the rewards even higher. And among those stakes were those belonging to the American viewing public, for TV was a fairly new medium in the late 1950s. Just as Americans were getting used to it enough to trust it, the quiz show scandals made them wonder if they ought to.

But all this hoopla quickly receded—in fact, it is hardly too much to say that it almost vanished overnight. This occurred not because Americans had grown tired of quiz shows—the drama of the sweltering, brilliant contestants who stewed over their answers under pressure was great TV. It was scandal that broke the hold of these quiz shows on the American viewing imagination. In the fall of 1958, former contestants came forward with allegations that the quiz shows were fixed—that contestants were provided the questions and answers in advance or otherwise given assistance to increase the show's dramatic tension—and the whole enterprise came tumbling down. Americans were stunned, even outraged. One network president resigned in disgrace, quiz show producers were banned from the industry for a time, and even more contestants admitted in tears or anger that they had received help.

When President Eisenhower, previously addicted to *The $64,000 Question*, learned about the quiz show scandals, he wondered aloud what had happened to the "national moral fiber."

For years after the scandals broke, the only game shows the networks allowed to continue were ones in which skills were absolutely unfixable (such as bowling) or in which ordinary klutzes did stunts against the requirements of an official clock in exchange for such modest gifts as a pair of new slacks (such as *Beat the Clock* on CBS and then ABC, which ran until 1961 on the networks). A glut of quiz shows in the mid-1950s was followed by a flock of Westerns later in the decade, where the only question that cowboys had to answer was "What ya drinkin', partner?" No doubt the Westerns, with their melodrama and transparent sense of right and wrong, white and black, were especially appealing after the corruption of the quiz shows.

THAT WAS THEN, THIS IS NOW: Isolation booths seem to have gone out of favor as a standard feature in quiz shows today. The most recent popular show of this type, *Who Wants to Be a Millionaire*, eschewed them. Contestants did their dramatic thinking about answers out in the open, right across from the host. Apparently the producers thought putting them into glass booths would have been excessively melodramatic for a more ironic and skeptical age such as ours. Or maybe the very idea of "isolation" has a bad connotation today. Or perhaps in this age of digital multitasking in Starbucks, no one would believe that contestants actually needed privacy to think.

HYPOTHETICAL USAGE IN A SENTENCE BY THE OLD AND SETTLED: "Be quiet and do your math assignment, or I'll lock you in an isolation booth for the rest of your life." —A parent speaking to an unruly fifteen-year-old in 1956

JOHN BERESFORD TIPTON

THE
MILLION-DOLLAR
MAN

TIMELINE: *The Millionaire* was a television drama that ran on CBS from 1955 to 1960.

INSPIRED GUESS BY TODAY'S YOUNG AND RESTLESS: The president of Harvard about five hundred years ago.

THE ANCIENT TRUTH: John Beresford Tipton was the reclusive but eminently wealthy titular character on *The Millionaire*, and over the course of five years and 206 episodes, "the benefactor" gave nearly a billion (fictional) dollars away. The show aimed to explore human nature—specifically, how ordinary people would react to sudden and unexpected wealth and good fortune, such as if someone offered them a cashier's check for one million dollars with all taxes prepaid. This was the premise on which the show's ingenious script writers operated.

Actors both famous and near-famous played starring roles on the series. The sundry millionaires included both janitors and accountants, people who came from all walks of life. Their newfound wealth did not always make them happy and created just as many difficulties as it resolved. As JBT seemed to know already, human nature is of such complexity that a lot of money does not invariably bring everlasting joy. Perhaps this was the message the show hoped to impart to its many viewers.

Transfixed viewers never saw JBT other than his right arm. The show began in his palatial estate known as Silverstone. A vocal artist named Paul Frees, who later did voices on *The Rocky and Bullwinkle Show*, voiced JBT, whose playful baritone gave instructions to a cheerful but earnest emissary named Michael Anthony (played by actor Marvin Miller): "Here's our next millionaire, Mike. I want a full report." Mike would deliver the check to the shocked beneficiary and then vanish. The rest of the night belonged to the new millionaires.

Here are examples from the show's various weekly plots:

- *A prideful man won't marry his girlfriend until he's financially able to support her. He gets one million dollars, but he hasn't earned it. Should he go ahead and marry her now?*
- *A gypsy woman tries to use her million to break into high society. But will money alone be enough?*
- *The wife of a matador wants to use the million dollars to get her husband out of the dangerous bullfight ring. But suppose he loves his work?*

- *A milkman starts leaving champagne rather than milk on the door of a woman he's sweet on. But what will her reaction be?*
- *An older woman tries to use her million to revive her debutante days. But how can one million dollars erase her wrinkles?*

The program might have served to dampen class envy, for who knows what sorrow Rockefeller might have had, despite all his millions. But it was more likely an exercise in an American-style theology. JBT played a sort of passive deity, who set matters in motion and then sat back to watch, as if he were a god who gave his people chances, but then the rest was up to them. In that way, the show suggested that in the end, we have no one else to blame but ourselves. Ralph Waldo Emerson, a century before *The Millionaire* came on TV, warned that "a rise in rents" (or a million dollars) may make us *think* "good [things] are preparing for [us]." Emerson encouraged his readers not to believe it, for nothing can bring us peace or happiness but ourselves. This doctrine of self-reliance seemed to be the underlying message of *The Millionaire*.

THAT WAS THEN, THIS IS NOW: How would *The Millionaire* fare today? Given the popularity of reality television, it likely wouldn't do well. Today we frequently like our television shows to feel more authentic and feature true-to-life, ordinary people as they grapple with survival, love and family, fame, and fortune on shows like *Survivor, American Idol, Real Housewives*, and *Project Runway*. As for "the benefactor" character, today he'd be more likely to be giving his millions to a political super-PAC rather than to a nice man who could use a million bucks to get his innocent girlfriend out of prison.

HYPOTHETICAL USAGE IN A SENTENCE BY THE OLD AND SETTLED:

"Wow, thanks: I didn't know I was going out with John Beresford Tipton!" —One of your father's old girlfriends, after he only gave her a box of Tootsie Rolls on Valentine's Day in 1957

JUNGLE JIM

TARZAN WITH CLOTHES

TIMELINE: The *Jungle Jim* series began as a comic strip in 1934 and quickly moved to radio, followed by a TV and film series in the 1950s.

INSPIRED GUESS BY TODAY'S YOUNG AND RESTLESS: A celebrity zoo keeper on *The Late Show with David Letterman*.

THE ANCIENT TRUTH: Jungle Jim was a popular fictional character set in the jungles of both Southeast Asia and Africa. For over two decades (1934 to 1956), this big-game safari hunter was the subject of comic strips, radio, movies (Saturday serials), comic books, and finally TV. Jungle Jim became a brand name, like McDonald's or Walmart today. Every boy adored Jim Bradley, a man of resources, justice, toughness, good humor, and high ethics. In addition to the physical challenges of facing wild beasts, craven ivory hunters, and atavistic natives, he also had to deal with femmes fatales and wicked cult women.

It is tempting to compare him to Tarzan, a more famous jungle action figure. This is partly because Johnny Weissmuller, the actor who played Tarzan in films throughout the 1930s and '40s, also played Jungle Jim. In spite of their differences (Jim was a professional hunter in Southeast Asia while the nearly naked Tarzan was the "king of the apes" living in the African jungle), there probably wouldn't have been a Jungle Jim without Tarzan, for it was Tarzan who first established the prototype of a comfortable, protective white hero in the jungle.

Both Tarzan and Jim fought to protect the jungle's right to be itself, free from marauders like poachers and miners. Both characters had to deal with the natural dangers of avalanches, floods, and poisoned darts. Both had mischievous chimps (Cheeta and Tamba, respectively) and special intuitive ties to animals, as when Tarzan talked to elephants or when protective gorillas rescued Jim. Yet for all this similarity, Jim and Tarzan are fundamentally different characters. Unlike Tarzan who preferred the jungle over civilization, Jim chose to be in the jungle only for a while. He is a liaison between the forces of civil order and the unique vagaries of the jungle. The Tarzan series was always more popular than the short-lived Jim TV series. Tarzan became mythic (movies, novels, television) in a way that Jim did not. This is because Tarzan's decision is more radically romantic and mysterious: he chose to become the king of the apes, while Jim was at best their occasional protector. Tarzan is the "natural man" at odds with the corruptions of civilized life; Jim is just an animal rights guy. But both of them were great fun.

THAT WAS THEN, THIS IS NOW: Jungle Jim would not do today. He is the big white bwana lording it over the African natives, however benevolently, so although he often fights bad white guys, he reeks of imperialism. Africa, too, continues to grow and evolve; it is also becoming the continent of skyscrapers and to outsiders, is no longer just about exotic darkness. Jungle Jim would be laughed out of the Congo.

HYPOTHETICAL USAGE IN A SENTENCE BY THE OLD AND SETTLED:
"Who do you think you are—Jungle Jim?" —Mrs. Stewart, after coming home and catching Mr. Stewart teetering on a stepladder to find the booze she had hidden at the top of the cabinet, in 1953

#42 KING OF THE WILD FRONTIER

COONSKIN CAP

TIMELINE: Walt Disney brought Davy Crockett to life in a television series in the 1950s. There was also a popular film in 1955.

INSPIRED GUESS BY TODAY'S YOUNG AND RESTLESS: The subject of an article about a hiker and his equipment in the "Gear Guy" section of *Outside* magazine.

THE ANCIENT TRUTH: Davy Crockett was a nineteenth-century American folk hero, commonly referred to as the "king of the wild frontier." His legend was brought to television in a wildly popular miniseries, *Davy Crockett,* starring actor Fess Parker, which ran from 1954 to 1955 as a five-part serial on ABC's *Disneyland.*

Davy Crockett was a "craze" during its time, because it seemed that every child from the ages of five to twelve yearned for at least one Davy Crockett toy. The Davy Crockett merchandise included Davy's signature coonskin cap, plus lunch boxes, action toys, Kool-Aid glasses, and cap pistols, among many others. Even today, there is a lusty nostalgia market for vintage Davy Crockett merchandise. Buffs with a serious case of Davy longing can purchase coffee mugs, T-shirts, wall clocks (with the Alamo on the face), and coonskin-cap teddy bears.

The Disney star who played Crockett on the TV series, Fess Parker, opened a winery in California in which the logo on the labels was…a golden coonskin cap. The raccoon and grapes alike were very good to Fess Parker.

Davy Crockett was "king of the wild frontier" during a time when American Western heroes were both engaging and credible. The legends of the Old West had not yet been subjected to the historical scrutiny that appears on such factual and sometimes debunking programs as PBS's *American Experience*. The show thrilled viewers with a vicarious sense of adventure, the excitement of the unknown frontier, and the clash of man versus wild. In such unmapped terrain as the unsettled West, a sensational and precarious episode is ever a possibility, or so Disney would have had us believe. There were only five episodes in the *Davy Crockett* TV series, but Davy's adventures were numerous. Davy fought "Injuns" with General Andrew Jackson and river bandits with his friend Mike Fink. Armed with only a knife, he killed a bear. He died at the Alamo fighting Mexicans, but Disney wisely refrained from showing Davy dead; instead, the last we see of him, he's swatting away as many of General Santa Anna's armed troops as he can until the Texas Republic flag fills the screen as an homage to the wild frontier's greatest king.

Disney was always trying to replicate the profitable nuttiness of the Davy Crockett franchise. In addition to the paraphernalia, the studio tried lots of new heroic characters, including the casting of Leslie Nielsen (who later became legendary for telling an airline stewardess not to call him "Shirley" in the movie *Airplane*) as Francis Marion in a show called, not inappropriately, *Swamp Fox*. But the audience didn't fall for that.

THAT WAS THEN, THIS IS NOW: Today, the myths of the Old West

have lost their resonance for both parents and their youngsters. Low-tech Western heroes like Davy Crockett cannot compete with the sleek, fast-paced world of superheroes in blockbuster movies such as *Spiderman*, *X-Men*, *The Dark Knight*, *The Avengers*, and many others. Besides, frontiersmen killing Native Americans is a socially discouraged activity today. Disney's Davy Crockett was of a time and place that isn't coming back.

HYPOTHETICAL USAGE IN A SENTENCE BY THE OLD AND SETTLED:

"Please devote yourself to attaining the status of king of the wild frontier in the backyard, not the living room." —Timmy Wilson's father Chester, speaking to his rambunctious nine-year-old son (who had donned a raccoon cap) in Teaneck, New Jersey, 1955

"LET IT ALL HANG OUT"

MANTRA OF THE 1960S

TIMELINE: The one-hit wonder the Hombres recorded "Let It Out (Let It All Hang Out)" in 1967, which led to widespread use of the expression.

INSPIRED GUESS BY TODAY'S YOUNG AND RESTLESS: Chilling out in your bare bod—and everyone being okay with it.

THE ANCIENT TRUTH: "Let it all hang out" was a catchphrase of the countercultural 1960s, with its free-wheeling disdain for outmoded strictures and uptight moods. The expression essentially meant to relax rather than despair in the face of stress or pressure. While the musical group the Hombres didn't invent the phrase, they seized on it to create their hit single.

Nobody knows what it's all about.
It's too much, man, let it all hang out.

Famously, the Beatles put it a bit differently in 1970: let it be.

For many, "let it all hang out" was a core philosophy that, to some, suggested a serene indifference to the state of the world. In fact, young people were not indifferent to everything (like free dope, freely available sex, and rock 'n' roll), but were openly resistant to the values of their parents, who traditionally valued linear goals and upward mobility as a result of living through the Great Depression and World War II. Their children, who existed in a more prosperous America, spurned this rat race and the uptight attitudes that apparently went with it. Therefore, "let it all hang out" really translated to a tranquil disinterest in the conventional values of their parents.

> "Let it all hang out" also meant a frankness—a self-exposure— that equated any lack of candor with hypocrisy. This aspect of "letting it all hang out" laid the groundwork, about fifteen years later, for revealing talk shows such as *Oprah* and *Phil Donahue*.

THAT WAS THEN, THIS IS NOW: Today's millennials are indifferent to the idea of "let it all hang out" altogether. That's because the hippies of the late 1960s successfully ushered in a new era of social and sexual freedom. The phrase was new and radical in the '60s because it challenged the uptight, buttoned-up, and neo-Victorian culture of the postwar era. But now, most Americans let it all hang out every day without even knowing it. We wear pajamas on airplanes, confess our darkest secrets on reality television, and always speak our minds no matter the consequence. There's an old saying: "When you've sold, stop selling." "Let it all hang out" has stopped selling.

HYPOTHETICAL USAGE IN A SENTENCE BY THE OLD AND SETTLED:

"Our teenager tells us to 'let it all hang out,' but we can't think of anything to do that with." —Mrs. Josephine Madole, fifty-one, of Montclair, New Jersey, in 1971

#44

LIBERACE

THE
CANDELABRA
MAN

TIMELINE: The height of Liberace's popularity was in the 1950s and '60s, though he continued to perform regularly through the mid-1980s.

INSPIRED GUESS BY TODAY'S YOUNG AND RESTLESS: A minor European painter during the Renaissance.

THE ANCIENT TRUTH: Liberace was one of America's greatest and best-paid entertainers, peaking between about 1950 and 1970. Liberace was born in a Milwaukee suburb as Wladziu Valentino Liberace, of a Polish mother and Italian father. Friends called him Lee; family called him Walter. He became known to the world as Liberace, a single name like that of one of the gods, such as Zeus. Known for his brand of effeminate and showy schmaltz, Liberace was an odd hybrid of showman and pianist—but people loved him. He was mesmerizing on TV, in supper clubs, in stadiums, on records, in films, and in concert halls.

His musician father saw early on that his son was a prodigy in the manipulation of ivory keys on strings and made him practice with fervor. Though ridiculed for his lack of interest in sports, Liberace soon began to earn a decent living, even as a teen during the Great Depression, by performing all over Milwaukee at weddings, funerals, night clubs, polka classes, and on the radio. (He even played for strip clubs, a practice his conservative Catholic family hated.) In time, his high school classmates accepted him as an odd but rather endearing fount of humor.

> When he was just a kid, Liberace met the great Polish pianist Ignacy Paderewski backstage at a Milwaukee theater; the encounter made him more determined than ever to become accomplished in his own right. He did, but perhaps not in the way that Paderewski, an earnest concert pianist, might have wished for his young groupie.

Why was Liberace so appealing? His flexibility, for one thing: he could play Chopin but didn't mind playing florid arrangements of "Home on the Range" or "Beer Barrel Polka" too. Since classical music generally had a snob appeal, Liberace's more democratic approach was uniquely welcome. At a time in the 1950s when the American middle class, though often not college educated, wanted to acquire a middle-brow culture—they bought their kids *World Book* encyclopedias—Liberace was just the thing: the perfect blend of Bizet and showbiz, of Schubert and schmaltz. His TV show of the early '50s, pioneering with such techniques as a split screen, earned him more millions in syndication. He even developed a logo: a candelabrum on the piano, at once corny and classical.

Another reason millions loved him: he was a terrific showman. Liberace hardly minded making a spectacle of himself. He became interested in design and was meticulous about the lighting of his performances. He wore white tails and trousers, which made him sublimely visible from the balcony of concert halls. In time, he started wearing rings so big they almost seemed to rival small boulders and enough feathers to put any ostrich to envy. He was taken onstage in gaudy cars—he'd have had them gold laminated if he could have (and maybe he did!)—or lowered onstage like some campy deus ex machina. His finger and handwork on the ivories became increasing dexterous and daring.

By the late 1970s, his personal life was in decline. Although he continued to be a hit in some places, especially Las Vegas, it became impossible to fight off allegations that he was homosexual. (He was gay, but to admit it likely would have caused him to lose his devoted fan base.) Liberace contracted AIDS and died in 1987 at the age of sixty-eight.

THAT WAS THEN, THIS IS NOW: Today's young people would likely find the once-tantalizing mystery surrounding Liberace—is he or isn't he gay?—uninteresting. With young people growing increasingly tolerant of homosexuality, who cares anymore? But at the same time, millennials would likely recognize Liberace's over-the-top showmanship in current stars such as Lady Gaga, known for her outrageous stage costumes (she once wore a dress composed of raw meat) and bizarre but compelling performances. Millennials might also watch the 2013 film *Behind the Candelabra* about Liberace's adrenalized affair with his younger companion Scott Thorson. Michael Douglas as Liberace, and Matt Damon as Thorson, both earned kudos for their portrayals.

HYPOTHETICAL USAGE IN A SENTENCE BY THE OLD AND SETTLED:

"You'll never be the next Liberace unless you practice eight hours a day and earn enough to buy us a solid gold grand piano." —A wittier-than-usual mother, speaking to her nine-year-old son in New York City, about 1970

LIBERAL ANTICOMMUNISM

A POLITICAL DILEMMA

TIMELINE: The zenith of the liberal anticommunism movement occurred between 1946 and 1989 as a product of the Cold War.

INSPIRED GUESS BY TODAY'S YOUNG AND RESTLESS: A liberal who's against communism, though I don't know why anyone cares about communism anymore.

THE ANCIENT TRUTH: While the inspired guess is accurate, it doesn't tell the complete story. The truth is that "liberal anticommunism"—a term now nearly forgotten—was one of the staples of American political discourse in the 1950s through the 1980s, and behind it lay one of the thorniest, angriest struggles in American political history.

After World War II, there were anticommunists, and then there were *liberal* anticommunists. Conservatives were unapologetic about their anti-red sentiments. Communists, especially in the

Soviet Union and China, were collectivist, atheist, and anti–private enterprise. They believed in a classless social structure that was founded on a common ownership of factories, infrastructure, natural resources, and more. What was there for conservatives *not* to hate?

But American liberals had a problem because many of the "commie" ideas, such as redistributing the nation's wealth for greater equality among all, seemed both viable and appealing. Such communist associations weren't a problem at all during World War II, when Russia was an ally against Hitler and China had not yet gone red. But in the war's aftermath, the diplomatic landscape shifted drastically. And then liberals had a big problem indeed.

As early as 1949, it had become abundantly clear to all that Soviet Russia's leader Joseph ("Uncle Joe") Stalin might well be a dangerous madman with expansionist aims and a penchant for atomic war. Hence, liberals of the old New Deal stripe (who believed in economic equality) had to make a distinction: "Yes, we're liberals who believe in equality and big government, but that doesn't make us communists. We still believe in freedom of enterprise, speech, religion, and so forth." This would seem to be a simple point to make, but it turned out to be both nasty and complicated.

During what became known as the Red Scare, a veritable witch hunt for secret, treasonous communists erupted in the United States, born out of a fear of the spread of communism. These claims were made by conservative Republicans who believed that communists were even working for the federal government. In turn, liberal anticommunists argued that the accusations against innocent radical thinkers were an abridgment of civil liberties. This effectively allowed conservative Republicans to accuse liberals who did not take the threat of internal subversion seriously enough of being "soft on communism." Thus a "liberal anticommunist" was almost as dangerous as a communist, and it became a terrible stigma for liberals for nearly forty years.

Liberal anticommunists were then faced with a terribly convoluted explanation. This involved what we might call the "multiple but" problem. "We're liberals *but* anticommunists, *but* we don't agree with taking away the civil liberties of folks and we don't agree with radicals to our left who think fascists are a greater threat than commies are." You were like a kid who'd done something really foolish, like trading your new bike for an ice-cream cone, but you were trying to convince your skeptical and disapproving parents that your decision had been more complex than it might seem to be. For them, the word "but" was a nonstarter. And so it was for much of the American voting public in the 1950s and '60s. Accordingly, during that period, both Democrats and Republicans won the White House, but the two Democrats who did, Kennedy and Johnson, both felt it necessary to contrast their domestic liberalism with their inflexible anticommunist principles abroad. They made their anti-red views as simple and rigid as possible, and their wish to keep it that way—to oppose communism everywhere, even when it was only part of a civil war in Asia—helped lead to the unwinnable debacle that was Vietnam.

THAT WAS THEN, THIS IS NOW: In the end, only the cessation of the Cold War itself relieved liberals of their problems with articulating their anticommunism. Ronald Reagan, a conservative Republican, accepted effective Soviet surrender at the end of the 1980s. By 1988, the Soviet empire of godless public ownership and military dictatorship had virtually collapsed. The irony is that the conservative Reagan—once himself a liberal anticommunist—trusted the Soviet Union enough to negotiate with them over their demise. His own advisers thought the likable old guy was becoming "soft on communism" in his dotage. But his trust of the Soviets made it possible for today's young people to grow up in a world where the terrible tensions of the Cold War are a nonfactor—and to save them from having to hear any tortured explanations about "liberal anticommunism."

HYPOTHETICAL USAGE IN A SENTENCE BY THE OLD AND SETTLED:
"I'm like a liberal anticommunist: I'm strictly opposed to your mother-in-law, but I don't necessarily hope she falls off a cliff." —Anonymous, speaking in about 1959

#46 LISTEN TO THE WARM

POLITICAL POETRY

TIMELINE: Rod McKuen's most famous book of poems, *Listen to the Warm*, appeared in 1967.

INSPIRED GUESS BY TODAY'S YOUNG AND RESTLESS: The tag line of an ad trying to sell oceanfront property.

THE ANCIENT TRUTH: "Listen to the warm" is the best-known line of a poem written by a once-well-known poet named Rod McKuen. It was especially popular with the youth counterculture of the 1960s.

The poet muses about letting the heart open to permit a little hurt to enter, recalling old loves, and remembering a "fuzzy" time when he wanted both to love and be loved. And then the great climax: at times, he just lies down and lets himself "listen to the warm." This is a poetic device in which versifiers splice together two of the five senses—this time it is hearing and touch—and the beautiful unexpectedness of this pairing resonated with many readers. As a result, "listen to the warm" became one of the popular phrases to emerge from the 1960s. It tapped concisely into popular ideas among the hippies of that revolutionary time:

- *diving into the self*
- *locating self-esteem in ineffable sources of comfort*
- *discovering peace and passivity in a higher sphere*

These ideas were not just personal; they were also political. In 1965, another poet, Allen Ginsberg (who had also worked on the creation of **Bucky Beaver**), came up with the related idea of "flower power" against the war in Vietnam. Thus protesters were "armed" (nice pun) with thousands and thousands of embroidered flowers, which they gave out to bystanders. They proclaimed themselves, ergo, as lovers, not fighters; peacemakers, not warriors. Even women's underwear, getting skimpier all the time, was emblazoned with "LOVE" on the fabric. The choice of sunflowers and carnations was right out of McKuen. There was a fairly straight and flowery line between "listen to the warm" and nonviolent, passive protests against the war.

In time, Ginsberg and others realized that just giving out flowers to the crowd wasn't attracting enough attention, so something more confrontational occurred: the flower children put their flowers into the gun barrels of the National Guardsmen who were providing security during the protests. The message, not without a certain smugness, was "make love, not war." This application of flower power was captured most vividly by photographer Bernie Boston during the 1967 antiwar protest at the Pentagon in Washington, DC.

For all the tacit condescension and trendy pantheism of the hippies though, they turned out to be on the right side of history. Whatever American intentions may have been in Vietnam, it was widely thought of as an imperialistic war. Even Americans who supported the troops came to dislike the war itself and wonder if it had been a mistake, especially after the Americans' panicky exit in 1975. The associations of warm and fuzzy peace with free sex also turned out to be oddly prescient, for the birth control pill had made sexual intercourse less consequential in ways never seen before. So discredited was the idea of major incursions by the United States, the next prolonged American invasion of foreign countries (Afghanistan and Iraq) did not occur not until nearly thirty years after the Vietnam War ended. Earlier interventions—into Grenada (1983), Panama (1989), and Kuwait (Desert Storm in 1991)—were short-term affairs, and the responsible American presidents, fearful of repeating Vietnam-style quagmires, designed and executed them that way.

Even so, we've lost the rhetorical patina of flower power. The self-authenticating journey and inner pacifism of McKuen's *Stanyan Street and Other Sorrows* (1966) no longer resonates for a whole generation. Only old hippies think of peace in association with orchids any longer, and sex is just sex, not some subspecies of pantheism. We remain skeptical of foreign invasions and still enjoy our sexual freedoms. But we don't listen to the warm any more. The dandelion kids are gone.

THAT WAS THEN, THIS IS NOW: As for McKuen, today he is past eighty, and continues to write books of spiritual verse (his latest is called *A Safe Place to Land*). He remains a hero for some, in particular for those older Americans (Grandpa Hippies?) who think they had it right when they were twenty and see no reason to change now. In the latter part of his career, he has been more successful as a composer of songs, for which he's been nominated for two Academy Awards and one Pulitzer Prize. But his glory days as a leading poet of the counter-culture are over. His work is unmoored from the context in which he seemed to provide inspiration for a revolutionary youth movement.

HYPOTHETICAL USAGE IN A SENTENCE BY THE OLD AND SETTLED:

"If you don't stop reading that stuff, I'm going to toss it in the fireplace and let you 'listen to the warm' that way!" —Mr. Buford Byrnes, then fifty-five, exasperated in 1969 with his seventeen-year-old daughter's countercultural reading habits

#47

THE LONG BRANCH

DODGE CITY'S FINEST

TIMELINE: *Gunsmoke*, which introduced the world to the Long Branch Saloon, ran on CBS radio from 1952 to 1961 and on CBS TV from 1955 to 1975. Today it runs in syndication.

INSPIRED GUESS BY TODAY'S YOUNG AND RESTLESS: A GPS app for locating the nearest shade tree.

THE ANCIENT TRUTH: *Gunsmoke* was set in the 1870s Old West, and the watering hole served as Dodge City's unofficial town hall. The Long Branch was owned principally by Miss Kitty Russell and featured piano music, steak dinners, gambling, and drinks (mostly straight whiskey)—and it implicitly offered prostitution too. But the Long Branch was mostly where the show's four principal characters would meet to socialize and sometimes strategize about keeping some semblance of order and civilization in Dodge City. They were Marshal Matt Dillon (played on radio by William Conrad), embittered head of the town's constabulary; his unofficial deputy, most famously the eager but dense Chester Goode or the affable but slow-talking Festus Haggen; Miss Kitty herself; and the self-serving Doc Adams, the town's only physician. As the series went on and switched from radio to TV, with rangy and rugged James Arness as the iconic TV marshal, the Long Branch became less a house of ill fame and more a site of idle gossip and even civic virtue.

Gunsmoke is the longest-running dramatic series on television. *Law and Order* also ran for twenty years, but its 456 episodes cannot beat *Gunsmoke*'s 635. The longest-running nondramatic scripted show in television history is *The Simpsons* (twenty-five seasons, 544 episodes), but that's a cartoon, and any comparisons between Dodge City's Festus Hagen and Springfield's Homer Simpson—though both are a bit slow-witted—would surely be strained!

The essential formula for each show was always the same: crime and punishment, revenge and redemption—such as the jealous thespian who kills his rival, or the disturbed young man out to avenge the unjust hanging of his father. The radio production values were so superb that listeners felt they themselves were on the prairie, where horses could be heard cantering and dogs yelped faintly from somewhere far away. And then, especially in the TV version, there was the authenticity of the characters: the stoic, brave Matt; the ever-loyal Chester; the unpretentious but knowledgeable Doc; and the glamorous but straight-talking

Miss Kitty. *Gunsmoke* was never a sitcom, but it had the sitcom's feature of weekly "friends."

But the radio *Gunsmoke* was a darker place than the one on TV. On radio, there was perpetual talk of the violence, heat, sweat, and dust of the Old West. The characters took on embitterment about having to live out there. In comparison, Dodge City on TV was an optimistic, ever-evolving utopia, and the Long Branch was its cheerful headquarters. To be sure, the West was still portrayed as a rough place, not for the faint. And various characters (lots of guest stars over twenty years) brought their personal tales of woe and grudges to TV, just as they had to radio. But for audiences *watching* the four main characters together in the Long Branch—the marshal, the faithful deputy, the doc, and the saloon keeper—*their* Dodge City, which seemed to grow more civilized and progressive as the series went on, was set in the best of times—even an ideal time.

As *Gunsmoke* began on the radio in 1952, television was already beginning to dominate the older medium. That the show stayed on the radio until 1961 is remarkable (by then, radio was mostly talk and music) and is testament to how good it was. As for the TV series, it ran until 1975. The show's cast was shocked to learn that the series had been canceled—they had to read about it in the trade papers—because they had every reason to expect it to continue; after all, the series was still in the top thirty, if no longer number one.

THAT WAS THEN, THIS IS NOW: The popularity of the Old West passed quickly. Within thirty years of what was portrayed as Matt and Kitty's heyday, there was a six-story building in downtown Dodge City. But if the Old West skedaddled along, TV shows *about* the Old West just kept trotting on and on, though none has lasted longer than the pulp novel *Iliad* that once was *Gunsmoke*. Consider a brief comparison between *Gunsmoke* and the now-canceled *Deadwood* (2004–2006), the last TV Western that tried to become long-running. The former, a network show during a time when cable was unimportant, had to appeal to a more general audience, still enamored of a West supposedly divided between ruffians and marshals, while the latter, with a more narrow-cast cable audience (HBO), was free to portray how small South Dakota communities were prey to the greediness of Eastern capitalists and their ever-reliable instrument of power, the venal federal government they had in their back pockets. The former helped reinforce the myth of courageous lawmen, faithful blacksmiths, sturdy doctors, and canny but compassionate saloon owners; the latter aimed, for a smaller but more sophisticated audience, to replace the *Gunsmoke* myth with a countermyth: the West not as fight between outlaws and sheriffs, but between little people and the big robber barons who would filch their livings by ravaging the land on which they depended. *Gunsmoke* today is a reminder of when we had a less mordant view of what the Old West was all about.

HYPOTHETICAL USAGE IN A SENTENCE BY THE OLD AND SETTLED:

"Where do you expect me to find a doc this time of night—in the Long Branch?" —Eston Southampton, wondering what to do in rural Indiana when his wife complained of a severe stomachache, in 1959

LSMFT

SOLD, AMERICAN!

TIMELINE: Lucky Strike began marketing its cigarettes with the slogan in 1945 and continued throughout the 1950s and '60s.

INSPIRED GUESS BY THE YOUNG AND RESTLESS: Maybe some kind of new text speak, like "Let's Stop Messing with Friending and Texting"—but why haven't I heard of it before?

THE ANCIENT TRUTH: LSMFT meant "Lucky Strike means fine tobacco," a phrase that the American Tobacco Company coined in 1945 to sell Lucky Strike cigarettes. This was not the first commercial slogan the company used and hardly the first successful one. But it was, in historical terms, the final line that nearly every American came to associate with Lucky Strike. "Remember, folks: LSMFT—Lucky Strike means *fine* tobacco." The brand has ceased to be the great popular choice it once was, especially in the 1930s. Fewer Americans every year can tell you what LSMFT stood for.

The brand itself premiered as a post–Civil War chewing tobacco (something male saliva glands could treasure while the man himself might have been ruing the tragic war that had been). Like much else that occurred in booming America after the war seemed to settle the slavery issue, the brand also proved to be a very "lucky" discovery indeed. Although Lucky Strike moved on to cigarettes, they were thought to be effeminate until American "doughboys" began to smoke them between battles in the devastated French countryside in World War I. By the 1920s, cigarettes were perceived as eminently masculine, and their popularity skyrocketed. The American Tobacco Company, which by then had purchased Lucky Strike, then began to plot how to make the brand as popular as Camels, made by the R. J. Reynolds Tobacco Company. Their first lucky strike of advertising ingenuity came with the announcement that their tobacco was "toasted" rather than sun-dried. This was somehow supposed to imply a vital difference in quality and taste compared to the competition. Then there was the plot to get women to smoke Luckies with the slogan "reach for a Lucky instead of a sweet." In the 1930s when chic women wanted to be willowy thin and leggy, this advice seemed to be an excellent idea. Besides that, smoking a Lucky meant not only that you could stay girlishly trim, but also that you were sophisticated and "new." By the 1930s, Luckies had become a powerful national brand.

But American Tobacco wasn't sitting on any laurels of tobacco leaf. It then began a whole new series of commercials by which to take radio listeners to North Carolina tobacco auctions featuring an auctioneer named "Speed" Riggs, known for the rapidity of his speech in a business that required it. His "Sold, American," which came out as something like "soldmerican," became part of the national speech, just as LSMFT had. Here the proposition was that Lucky Strikes were not only toasted, fashionable, and slimming, but also that only the best tobacco was used in them.

LSMFT emerged during the last year of World War II and remained a staple of the company's ad campaigns for another thirty years. And it continued to promote its cosmopolitan weeds by sponsoring one of the most listened to musical programs on radio, *Your Hit Parade*. By the '40s, Lucky Strike had its own orchestra, which accompanied the singers on the weekly show, featuring the most popular songs in the land.

During World War II, American Tobacco declared itself patriotic by ending the green background of its label. "Lucky Strike green has gone to war," it said, claiming that copper had been required to make the green background but was needed now to defeat Hitler and Tojo. Surveys revealed that women didn't like the green background, and this provided American Tobacco with a noble excuse to get rid of it. The more appealing white background emerged and remained in place for years. The company also put the new label—Lucky Strike in red letters—on both sides of the carton.

In time, however, great advertising could no longer help. In the mid-1970s, a British firm acquired the Lucky Strike label. By then, the middle and upper-middle classes were starting to turn against cigarette smoking and in particular against unfiltered weeds. Warnings about the health hazards of smoking from such authorities as the surgeon general of the United States and the requirement that such admonitions be put on cigarette packages were decidedly unhelpful to the cause of tobacco sales. The link between what Johnny Carson, toward the end of his rich but carcinogenic life, called "those damned cigarettes" and lung cancer was unbreakable in the public consciousness. Purists continued—and still continue—to smoke the "fine" and "toasted" tobacco of Lucky Strikes, which expanded into menthol and "light" versions. They have not been a super-popular brand, however, for many years.

THAT WAS THEN, THIS IS NOW: LSMFT has gone the way, in a sense, of the cigarette itself. While many people continue to smoke cigarettes, smoking no longer has the cultural cache it once did. Cigarettes are now thought addictive and unhealthy. Tobacco company ads are strictly regulated. Today's younger people have never seen a cigarette commercial on television. They must wonder at all the lit smokes that cloud the scenes in *Mad Men.* These days, workers are asked to go outside if they want to "commit" smoking. Today's slogan might be LSMED: Lucky Strike means early death. Perhaps the new high-tech (and supposedly safe) electronic cigarettes will resuscitate the bad habit—too soon to tell. Yet many young people, year after year, continue to find cigarette smoking cool. That, explains bestselling social science author Malcolm Gladwell, is not so much because the practice of smoking itself is cool but that *people* who smoke are cool. It's the smokers who are chic, not the smoking. Public service ads warning against the dangers of smoking may, paradoxically, lead *more* young people to smoke—because to do so is perilous and thus attractively rebellious.

HYPOTHETICAL USAGE IN A SENTENCE BY THE OLD AND SETTLED:

"I can't stand the smell of your smokes. Why don't we just say that LSMFT means 'let's stop making frigging tobacco!'?"—The boss of Wally Spurlock, a Lucky addict, just before Wally's "immediate supervisor" told him to cut down to a half a pack a day while on the job

MADE IN JAPAN

A
DEMEANING
LABEL

TIMELINE: The denigrating label was commonplace in the United States during the first seven years after World War II.

INSPIRED GUESS BY TODAY'S YOUNG AND RESTLESS: Something made in Japan, like a car, which means that it's better than autos made in the United States.

THE ANCIENT TRUTH: "Made in Japan" was a label stamped on Japanese products between 1945 and 1952, during the period when the United States occupied Japan as a conquered enemy. Sometimes the label said "Made in Occupied Japan" and the adjective counted a lot, for every time Americans bought such a product, they could do so with the satisfactions of military triumph. After Japan's surprise attack on the American naval base at Pearl Harbor in Hawaii in 1941—which propelled the United States into World War II—American hatred of the Japanese was even greater than that directed toward Hitler, who had not launched an attack on American soil. In 1945, the United States dropped atomic bombs on the cities of Hiroshima and Nagasaki, which ultimately left over two million Japanese dead. (Even years later, cancer from the radiation fallout continued to terminate lives.) This effectively brought an end to World War II, and the Japanese surrendered to the Allies about a week later.

Part of the resulting trade agreement between the United States and Japan was that the Japanese could export products to the United States as long as they were labeled "Made in Occupied Japan," later just "Made in Japan." It was a way to allow the Japanese to make and export goods, but also allow wary American consumers to make informed decisions about their purchases. Americans tended to view Japanese-made items as inferior to those made in Europe—yet the items were cheap and unusual curiosities that nevertheless had a market: green chintz teacup sets, small painted dishes, flowery lemon servers, pink sugar and creamer sets, dessert bowls decorated with spring violets, and porcelain statuettes with a saxophone-playing bunny, to name a few.

Some Americans purchased these products in a spirit of gloating condescension. Others no doubt thought that buying these products would contribute to the Japanese payment of war reparations. Perhaps others, with a little more kindness in their bosoms, thought it was a way of forgiving a people whose land Americans had, after all, devastated. After the war, Japanese cities were nothing but skeletal cinders, and its crop fields were ashen.

"Made in Occupied Japan" was partly an abject plea: "Buy from us in spite of all that we have done to you." And Americans between 1945 and 1952 could surely afford to look with superiority at the tiny Japanese figurines on sale at "dime stores" such as Woolworth's, especially when victorious America's share of the world's gross production was several times greater than its leading competitors in the realm of nations.

"Made in Japan" was a humiliating end to the once-proud Japanese military. Since the early twentieth century, the Japanese had longed to be an imperialistic power, but during the '30s and '40s, the United States, which had its own interests in the Pacific, was standing in the way. The Japanese invasion of China was especially galling to public opinion in the United States. As a protest against far-flung Japanese conquests, the United States froze Japanese assets and stopped selling the Japanese the oil and scrap iron they needed to continue their ambitions—which was a contributing factor to Japan's decision to bomb Pearl Harbor. They were emboldened by how much the United States had reduced its armaments during the Depression and by the success of their ally, Hitler, in Western Europe.

THAT WAS THEN, THIS IS NOW: Obviously the old connotation of "Made in Japan"—flimsy, cheap, and something Americans will buy just because we feel sorry for the people over there—is gone for good. Exports are the lifeblood of the Japanese economy, and its products are now widely perceived to be innovative and high quality. In particular, Japan is known for sterling brands such as Toyota and Honda automobiles, Sony and Toshiba electronics, as well as medical equipment, rubber, plastics, and even organic chemicals. In fact, Japan was the world's number four exporter in 2012. Meanwhile, "Made in Occupied Japan" products remain in demand as valuable vintage collectibles and can be found aplenty on eBay.

HYPOTHETICAL USAGE IN A SENTENCE BY THE OLD AND SETTLED:

"Dad's convictions are so flimsy you'd think they were made in Japan." —Peggy Audrey, seventeen, in 1950, on how easily she can persuade her father to let her do just about anything

MILTOWN

TRANQUILITY FOR THE NATION

#50

TIMELINE: It went on the market as America's first blockbuster psychotropic pharmaceutical in 1955 and was taken off the market in 1970.

INSPIRED GUESS BY TODAY'S YOUNG AND RESTLESS: A hip reference to Milwaukee, Wisconsin.

THE ANCIENT TRUTH: Miltown was the brand name for meprobamate (meh-PRO-bah-mate), the most popular tranquilizer used by Americans in the 1950s. By 1957, one-third of all American prescriptions were written for the stuff. It acquired the nickname "Mommy's little helper," as it enabled moms to cope with unruly toddlers and (even worse) the fear of nuclear annihilation in the 1950s, sometimes dubbed "the Age of Anxiety."

In an America dotted with split-level homes with bomb shelters in the backyard, you'd want to know where your Miltown was in case you had to take it with you underground while you waited out whatever atomic rocket exchange the Soviet Uncle Joe (Stalin) and the American Uncle Sam might have gotten up to. Miltown was thought to forestall a "nervous breakdown," a catch-all term for any form of serious mental disorder.

> The comedian Milton Berle thought the pill so effective that he said his name should be "Miltown" Berle.

It was vital for the makers of Miltown to claim, plausibly, that it was a relaxant (or tranquilizer) rather than a sedative. A "sedative" would make you sleepy, while a "tranquilizer" would make you calmer so you could be more alert and productive. If it were a sedative, then it might make you dangerously unresponsive and, in higher doses, lead to coma or death. So Miltown, its makers declared, was in no way a sedative. But in time, that is precisely how Miltown came to be regarded.

In truth, it didn't take much of an overdose to create chancy side effects, such as drowsiness. Miltown is thought of as crude compared to today's mood enhancers: their alteration of the central nervous system is much more sophisticated. Miltown, though its users tried to think of it as an overall improver of mood, was really just a downer. Intended to be a mood enhancer, it turned out to be a depressant. By the 1960s, it became more heavily regulated by the federal government. By 1970, it was listed as a controlled substance by the Food and Drug Administration, which proclaimed that it created unhealthy physical and psychological dependence. (A modern-day example of this would be the powerful painkiller Vicodin.) In 2012, the European Union banned its primary ingredient altogether. Now it has largely entered the hermetically sealed chambers of lost history.

It is impossible to know how much good or harm it did back in the 1950s. To some, it did a lot of harm. They got hooked on it. But for others, it may have meant the difference between spanking your kid or not, or between quitting your impossible job or staying with it a bit longer for the sake of the family. Its true importance really dwells in how it entered a larger drama in American life. This drama came in two parts.

Part one involved the very idea of taking a drug to improve your life rather than to cure an illness. Americans have often been a puritanical and self-denying people. The very idea of taking a pill just to feel better, as opposed to taking one to cure your sinus infection or relieve your aching back, was a notion that only took hold among Americans in the 1950s, the decade after America had won the war and deserved, some thought, to relax a little. But it was an idea at war with the pervasive American fear of softness and decadence. Because kitchen-bound women in the '50s were less caught up in this dilemma—easy street versus hard work—they took more Miltown than the guys did. As for men, they had to be convinced that Miltown would make them more productive rather than less. Some thought, for a while, that it did.

Part two involves the American inconsistency about drugs in general. This part of the drama started in the 1960s, when young people began to experiment with illicit drugs. This was not many years after such countercultural figures as Aldous Huxley maintained that mind-altering drugs were the "white powdered road to the future." Parents were aghast at all the pot and LSD, and their children were aghast that their parents would say anything negative at all after they had been splurging on Miltown for ten years or more. Thus Miltown and other "life-enhancing" drugs seemed to millions of hippies as just a legalized version of what they themselves were craving and ingesting. This critique has never entirely gone away, as Americans' attitudes toward drugs are often caught on the hypocrisy of a nation that drinks a lot of alcohol but conducts a war on coke. Charges of such contradiction remain a staple of countercultural and libertarian discourse to this very day.

THAT WAS THEN, THIS IS NOW: Miltown was eventually replaced with much more effective mood enhancers with fewer side effects. Today's Lexapro and Prozac let you have it all—though they don't work equally well for every person's biochemistry, and long-term effects remain under study. In addition, the broader conditions that made Miltown appealing—bored housewives stuck at home with gleaming appliances and high-strung 1950s kids, or anxious citizens afraid of the bomb—no longer exist. Today we live in a harried age, but we do not dread utter extinction in the same way that those living under the threat of nuclear war did. Yet in another sense, Miltown has won, because pills for the head are beginning to trump talking to the shrink as a cure for mental problems. We're just a bit too busy, it seems, and why bother with therapy when there's such a quick fix available?

HYPOTHETICAL USAGE IN A SENTENCE BY THE OLD AND SETTLED: "I wonder if I might check in to the Miltown Motel and let you watch these incorrigible kids for a couple of weeks." —Mrs. Maurer, thirty-nine, speaking to Mr. Maurer, in 1960

MIMEOGRAPH

#51

BEFORE THERE WAS XEROX

TIMELINE: Mimeographs date back to the late nineteenth century and only got better and more affordable as the twentieth century went on. But by the 1960s, Xerox copier machines were beginning to replace them.

INSPIRED GUESS BY TODAY'S YOUNG AND RESTLESS:
A new app that lets you alter your own photo so you look like a celebrity, such as Miley Cyrus.

THE ANCIENT TRUTH: The mimeograph was the primary means of mechanical reproduction in offices and schools during the mid-twentieth century. Nearly everyone over the age of forty will remember them. Once upon a time, they seemed fairly high-tech. The mimeograph machine was invented by the genius Thomas Edison in 1876 and licensed a decade later by one A. B. Dick, who also coined the term. Among its competitors in the battle of the copying machines were the spirit duplicator and the Thermo-Fax, each of which used different techniques. Yet it was Xerox that drove the mimeo out of existence. The odd thing about the Xerox revolution is that the technology of the *older* copying machine is far more interesting than that of the newer. The Xerox, which used a camera, was merely the latest chapter in a technology Americans had been following for years. Americans had seen advances in photography, from flashbulbs to quickly developing Polaroid film. So the evolution of photography to the point where it could snap a photo of a typewritten sheet of paper was only a matter of time.

Americans knew how Xerox machines worked: they saw the flashing light exposure by which the camera was able to take a picture of the original. But how did the "mimeo" work? You typed or drew on the original: a white sheet of paper stuck to a second sheet of blue ink, which everyone referred to as the stencil. Once you finished writing or typing on the original, you detached it from the blue-inked stencil and attached it to a drum, rolled it over and over again, and voilà! In a matter of seconds, your original, in vivid blue ink, *somehow* came tumbling through in multiple copies.

How did it manage to do so? The all-blue stencil was coated with waxed mulberry juice. As your typewriter or pen made indentions in the blank page, it was cutting little holes in the stencil. The drum forced ink through the holes in a manner that corresponded to your typewritten patterns. Amazing! Of course, every stencil had only a certain amount of waxed mulberry, so in time, the copies got fainter. It was always vital not to expect too many copies. But in effect, the mimeograph machine was a cheap printing press that frog-marched stencil ink onto sheets of paper. Those tiny holes made with your typewriter key or pen (or pencil) were performing little miracles of replication.

This was also an inconvenient process by today's digital standards. With mimeographs, you got ink on your hands. If you made a mistake on the original document, you sometimes had to use a small razor blade to make corrections—such as nicking away an undesired "e." But it was the vital difference between, say, a "bad cut" and the nonsensical "bad cute." Since it was possible to cut yourself on the razor blade, red blood often comingled with the waxen mulberry, a sickening prospect. By 1951, there were correction fluids (like Liquid Paper) that did the job of copyediting much more safely.

THAT WAS THEN, THIS IS NOW: Mimeograph machines have been replaced by electronic scanners today. Still, there are mimeograph machines being made for those who yet require or prefer inked stencils. In an uncanny melange of new and old technology, some of them even have scanners now, plus a thermal head for turning the images into inked copies. One of them is called a Risograph. But barring a severe energy shortage and therefore a catastrophic decline in electrical power, the old hand-cranked "mimeo" isn't making a comeback. If it does, we'll know we're in trouble. The mimeograph will always stand as an important chapter in the history of copying, but today's millennials would see its dependence on paper as a relic of times past.

HYPOTHETICAL USAGE IN A SENTENCE BY THE OLD AND SETTLED: "Mimeo that memo, would you? And don't cut yourself this time!" —The boss to his secretary at the Acme Office Supply Company in about 1959

#52 THE ORIGINAL AMATEUR HOUR

AN *AMERICAN IDOL* FOR ITS TIME

TIMELINE: *The Original Amateur Hour* debuted on the radio in 1934 and lasted until 1945. It was revived in 1948 as a TV show, where it ran until 1970.

INSPIRED GUESS BY TODAY'S YOUNG AND RESTLESS: The current Congress, or just incompetent management in general.

THE ANCIENT TRUTH: *The Original Amateur Hour* was America's first great amateur talent show, the predecessor of such popular attractions as *Star Search*, *America's Got Talent*, and *American Idol*. But in many instructive respects, *The Original Amateur Hour* was quite different.

It was first called *Major Bowes' Amateur Hour*, which began on radio in the 1930s. Major Edward Bowes was a man of military bearing (though the provenance of his military title has been debated) and no-nonsense impatience on the air. Someone said he had a gift for "nongab." He lost his fortune in the San Francisco earthquake of 1906 and, following his misfortune, came east to New York City, where, after producing some Broadway shows from 1911 to 1913, he took ownership and management of the Capitol Theater, from which he operated his radio show of nonprofessional talent. Although behind the scenes, Major Bowes may have tried to put his contestants at ease, on the show his "all right, all right" displayed an urgency to get on with the act and became the subject of nationwide mocking. But he had something far more lethal than just impatience.

He also had a large gong as a cue for the losing act to get offstage fast. Millions of listeners delighted, openly or secretly, in the rude and ringing way in which Major Bowes adjudged that—after all, amateur was amateur. During the Depression, it was sometimes fun to laugh at someone who, at least temporarily, was more humiliated than you were. (Schadenfreude at the disappointments of others has not entirely gone away, as the popularity of today's reality TV shows may suggest.) But in 1936, the major got rid of the gong because too many listeners told him it was an act of weekly perfidy.

The Original Amateur Hour was an extreme twist on the "variety show" (also see **Really Big Shew**). Opera singers, banjo players, those who might have played the harmonica while standing on their heads, five-year-old dancers, and those who could imitate virtually any musical instrument (or bird): all were part of a somewhat dubious feast each week. Some had genuine brilliance, including Frank Sinatra, who, with the Hoboken Four, appeared on the show numerous times, and Ann-Margret. People voted via what today we call "snail mail" (Box 191, Radio City Station, New York 2, New York) to urge that this or that act be brought back.

The major died in the mid-1940s, and the show was almost

immediately taken over by a talent scout and promoter named Ted Mack. If Bowes might have made contestants nervous, Mack went to great lengths to make them feel calm and assured. He had a genial, soothing way of talking that worked wonders to balance the bewildering array of talent—or lack thereof— that surrounded him. Despite the "hour" in the title of the show, it generally ran for only thirty minutes. It was one of a pocketful of programs that managed to run on all four major networks, including the soon-to-be-defunct DuMont. The show failed to reach younger audiences and declined in popularity.

While it is true that the amateur-hour-type programs were popular, the shows never attained the unbridled popularity of today's *American Idol*. (Even after more than ten seasons, the show still attracts millions of viewers.) Why not? The most obvious answer is that there are millions more TV sets—and watchers—now than there were when *The Original Amateur Hour* enhanced the tube. Another answer is that *American Idol* has celebrity judges, with their quick and acerbic wit. Yet another is that the contestants on *American Idol* do big acts, complete with high-production-value sets and a full orchestra; this big spectacle puts to shame the simple bare stage used by Bowes and Mack. And last, the prospects for someone or something "going viral" are far greater in the digital age than they were back then, so a Clay Aiken can truly soar to the summit in a matter of minutes. *American Idol* audiences can vote on the Internet or via mobile devices; *The Original Amateur Hour* audiences mostly voted with postcards and letters, a much slower process that did not lend itself to becoming an instant media sensation.

The prizes on *The Original Amateur Hour* were comparatively modest: maybe a $2,000 scholarship (worth about $18,000 today) if you won three weeks in a row, or maybe a chance to join the *Amateur*

Hour tours of such cities as Rock Island, Illinois, or Bangor, Maine. On the other hand, the prize for *America's Got Talent* has been one million dollars. It's a different country now.

But Major Bowes has left us with a quirky legacy, and that is *The Gong Show*, a zany mid-'70s program inspired by Major Bowes's instrument of exile. *The Gong Show* featured celebrity judges who often gonged "talent" out after only thirty seconds. Sometimes they were so eager to do so that they did so at the same time; this was called "gang-gonging." The entire show was founded on a mixture of absurdity and sadism. The acts were incredibly awful, including the "Popsicle Twins," two scantily clad young ladies whose act consisted of consuming their Popsicles in a suggestive manner. *The Gong Show* was eventually canceled and then syndicated. Until Jerry Springer came along, it won the Unofficial Bad Taste Award.

There was a rumor of unknown origin in the early '40s that someone on Major Bowes's program was giving out secret information to the Nazis in the form of codes (based on the dialogue of the show). It was alleged that every time the show aired, an American war vessel was sunk. Few believed the scurrilous accusation anyhow.

THAT WAS THEN, THIS IS NOW: Amateur hours are not unknown on TV today, as *American Idol* and *Dancing with the Stars* can attest. But while the contestants on the earlier show were catch-as-catch-can—with the occasional one actually becoming a star—the rivals on *American Idol* are *primed* to become stars. America's taste for so-so dancing accordionists has waned, it seems. We want stars and idols much more instantly. Perhaps this is in accord with our general impatience about images and information. Anyhow, the old, more spontaneous *Amateur Hour* is destined to remain in the dustbins of historical curiosities, even if it did give Pat Boone his first big break. One thing, however, has not changed. Major Bowes had his perfidious gong, while *Britain's Got Talent* has its acerbic judge, Simon Cowell.

HYPOTHETICAL USAGE IN A SENTENCE BY THE OLD AND SETTLED:

"If Mrs. Foley sings 'I Love You Truly' for one more wedding in that nasal voice of hers, I'm going to send her to *The Original Amateur Hour* just to get her out of town." —Pastor Winston Walts, speaking to his wife in 1948

PERCY DOVETONSILS

POET
FOR THE
AGES

#53

TIMELINE: The heyday for Ernie Kovacs's laughable poet Percy was 1952 to 1956, when Kovacs had a daily TV show called *The Ernie Kovacs Show.*

INSPIRED GUESS BY TODAY'S YOUNG AND RESTLESS: The name of a Disney cartoon character.

THE ANCIENT TRUTH: Percy Dovetonsils was a well-known fictional character created and played by the comedian Ernie Kovacs in the late 1950s. Percy had characteristics of a 1950s homosexual stereotype: poetry loving, narcissistic, vain, pretentious, and effeminate. He lisped, sported an outrageous zebra coat, displayed with dramatic overkill a skinny, long cigarette holder, and donned eyeglasses with Coke-bottle lenses, on the underside of which were painted eyes—all of this topped by elaborate spit-curled hair. Harp music cued his entrée, which simply found him sitting in an armchair. Percy resided on this outsize cushion, martini with daisy stirring stick at his side, and read his verse from an enormous book (his official occupation was "poet laureate"). Percy spoke in the syrupy voice of Sylvester the Cat, but in more of Percy's baritone than of Sylvester's tenor. He wrote and spoke ditties about how Mona Lisa never laughs aloud because she has bad teeth or how flies can get sinus trouble if they sit in martini ice too long.

Kovacs smoked a cigar underwater yet managed to blow smoke (it was milk he'd held in his mouth until the uncanny moment). He did a parody of *The Howdy Doody Show* set in Hungary (Kovacs was Hungarian American) with a totalitarian host called "Buffalo Mikos," who cut the strings of the annoying star puppet (Howdy Dee-Dee) in order to shut him up. He devised a musical threesome of apes (the Nairobi Trio), one of whom hit the other apes as often as he hit his cymbals.

This depiction of an obviously homosexual poet plays into every stereotype. Today it would be as offensive as **Amos 'n' Andy** would be. It would be regrettable if Kovacs were remembered only this way, because he was always a fervent experimenter. He was an acclaimed and popular comic—and extremely avant-garde. The early days of television, before standards and practices were set in concrete, gave him the opportunity to experiment. He put on a version of *Swan Lake* with ballerinas in gorilla suits. He did a video of a poker game accompanied by Beethoven's Symphony no. 5. (Kovacs adored classical music.) He portrayed himself as "Mr. Question Man" and answered a schoolboy's question—"if the earth is round, why don't more people fall off"—by stating that people are falling off all the time. He put on an expensive visual gag in which he played a car salesman who closed the hood of a model only to have it fall through the floor. This stint cost NBC $12,000 (over $100,000 today).

Kovacs once said of himself that he was born to a Hungarian family in Trenton, New Jersey, and smoked his first of innumerable cigars when he was an infant. He who was always ahead of the curve in comedy got ahead of another curve once too often, and in 1962, he crashed his car into a Santa Monica power pole. He was thrown halfway from the car and died in an instant. A cigar was found nearby. Perhaps he had been trying to light it. He was forty-three.

Now he mostly resides in oblivion. His second wife, comedienne Edie Adams, used his life insurance policy to buy back many of his videos, and in 2010, she used them in a TV special on ABC. It was the first time Kovacs had appeared on television in over four decades.

THAT WAS THEN, THIS IS NOW: Ernie Kovacs was such a comic genius—and had such an uncanny sense of what was funny and weird at once—that he might be a sensation for today's millennials, especially if he did political satire on Comedy Central. One can imagine him mimicking Senator Ted Cruz as he read *Green Eggs and Ham* to his kids on the Senate floor. But Kovacs would need to leave the character of Percy behind. The figure of the aesthetic snob is not as resonant or commonplace today as it was in the 1950s, but it would still be perceived as offensive and distasteful now.

HYPOTHETICAL USAGE IN A SENTENCE BY THE OLD AND SETTLED: "Who wrote this stuff—Percy Dovetonsils?" —Mr. Alvin Grange, speaking to his young son while reading *The Cat in the Hat* to him in 1958

#54 QUEEN FOR A DAY

WEEPY WEEKDAY CHARITY

TIMELINE: *Queen for a Day* ran on the radio from 1945 to 1957 and on TV from 1956 to 1964. It was revived briefly in the 1970s.

INSPIRED GUESS BY TODAY'S YOUNG AND RESTLESS: Sounds like an old movie about some European monarch, trampled to death by wild horses on the very day she became queen.

THE ANCIENT TRUTH: *Queen for a Day* was a popular daytime radio and television show that ran continuously on one medium or the other for nearly twenty years. The format of each episode was based on five women from ordinary life who told the show's moderator about their current run of bad luck. Toward the end of the show, the audience would applaud for each of them, the decibels registered on an "applause meter" that registered the crowd's enthusiasm on a horizontal scale. The woman with the loudest applause would win. This meant the show's sponsors would meet her special needs, thus turning her sad story into a happy ending.

It sounds simple, but beneath such a seemingly straightforward formula was one indispensable technique. While *Queen for a Day* (henceforth, *QFAD*) was a fine daily charity, there was always a clear distinction between the needy and the "truly needy." While the following account exaggerates, it always seemed that one contestant might ask for an extra maid, while another might request a new pair of Easter Sunday shoes. The final contestant might say that she had one child with polio, a husband on disability, and a cocker spaniel that hadn't eaten in two days. There was never any real doubt as to who the winner should be.

Then, to the strains of "Pomp and Circumstance," this woman was deemed "Queen for a Day"—the most frequent and long-running host, Jack Bailey, had been a World's Fair barker and had the booming voice required for such royal proclamations. She was crowned and given a red coat with sable lining to wear. (The sable mother who might have pleaded that her furry son be spared was never given an audience on the show.) She sat on a throne and heard that her special needs would be met. Her little boy would get the best treatment. Her husband would receive a lifetime pension. She would get two years' supply of Ken-L Ration dog food. She would get a fancy vacation, gleaming new appliances, several nights on the town, and new clothes (usually from the fashions featured on the show). She would also get many other goodies, but let us quit before we perish from excess giggles or tears, depending upon viewpoint.

At the program's end, Jack would sign off by averring that he wished we could make every woman queen for a day, every single day.

This teary desire only served to reinforce the economic realism that lay behind all the sappiness: so much need, so few resources.

Critics said the show was maudlin and tasteless, and so it was. At times, it was made even more so by the occasional addition of ponies and clowns to the set. Clothes makers, by making sure that Jack Bailey mentioned their brands as gifts for the new queen, shamelessly hawked their wares to stay-at-home women viewers, some of whom already had plenty of maids but who could indulge in the self-congratulation of pitying poor women who didn't. This was a clever way of advertising, because the brands, such as Nardis of Dallas, didn't have to pay for a formal commercial—they only needed to donate the dresses and get the plug as they were being distributed to that day's deserving queen. However, in the 1970s, it was revealed that the show was fictional and that all of the female contestants were actresses. Thus what appeared to be a reality show turned out to be just a fictional soap opera, and viewers felt cheated.

THAT WAS THEN, THIS IS NOW: *QFAD* would not be totally alien to young audiences in the new millennium. Today's Gen Y is a fairly liberal generation, aware of impoverishment and income inequality in the world. They would not object to a show that helped people out. But they would object to the teary sentimentality of the show. If this is a compassionate generation, it is also an ironic one. They would see right through the way the show was rigged. They might think that a government program or large foundation, not a schmaltzy televised charity, is the proper way to help the poor. Finally, the women in the '50s and '60s who went on the show were not working women partly because relatively few women worked back then—this was part of their perceived economic distress. The reality is that today's impoverished working women would not be able to get off work to go on *QFAD*.

HYPOTHETICAL USAGE IN A SENTENCE BY THE OLD AND SETTLED:

"Queen for a day? I'd just like to be queen for a minute!" —Your great-aunt talking, in a moment of extreme frustration, to her lazy husband in 1957

#55 RABBIT EARS

BEFORE CABLE

TIMELINE: In cities from the late 1940s until the 1990s, they were the preferred way of getting a TV signal. But the rise of cable television has rendered this device unnecessary for the majority of American viewers today.

INSPIRED GUESS BY TODAY'S YOUNG AND RESTLESS: Mr. Spock's earlobe malfunction in the original *Star Trek*.

THE ANCIENT TRUTH: Atop the TV sets of the '50s and '60s, the dipole (the simplest of all antennas for receiving electromagnetic signals) was called rabbit ears because the two antenna wires stuck up in the air like two long ears. The two wires fed into a driven element, an electrically connected receiver, equipped with what engineers uncannily called a "parasite," designed to make sure you got the signals of proper frequency and length from the broadcasting station.

But on occasion, the desperate TV watcher—eager for better reception so he could watch comedian Groucho Marx insult guests on *You Bet Your Life* or see pianist **Liberace** coo with his brother George over what a great Polish mother they had—might try putting the wires closer together or even at 180 degrees from each other. This was considered radical, but desperate times called for desperate measures, and back in those days, TV viewers were desperate to see the fast-talking comedian and the fast-playing pianist-showman.

Behind these machinations was the bitterest truth, though few back in those prehistoric days wished to admit it: TV reception was often not good at all. Only the most local stations could be received, and even those might fade on a cloudy or stormy day. Everyone cursed "snow," the static interference on the screen that ruined many an evening of *Dragnet*. Some poor souls even put aluminum foil on the tops of the wires to improve the reception.

Yet if you had a detached home, you could do better than rabbit ears. You could purchase and set up an outside antenna. Indeed, all over America, the size of your outside antenna was a great status indicator. Some middle-class people were finally able to move up from rabbit ears to simple, low-flying devices of skinny wires on their single-story roofs. Upper-class individuals had either high, billowing, silver antennas on top of their mansions or (even better) a tall, latticed steel stand stuck into their lawns (which always looked as though they'd just returned from an elite beauty parlor), on top of which was a soaring, magnificent, hubristic TV antenna. The mythical Icarus, with his fantastic wings made of wax, had nothing on these giant receivers. They were even better than Icarus, because only a tornado or hurricane, and not simply the heat of the sun, would bring them down.

One could rotate these outdoor antennas through a box on top of the set. Rotate to the left for stations to the south or west, to the right for stations to the north or east. You could hear the antenna with its whirring on the roof as it switched directions, like the pleasant sound of a robot doing precisely what you ordered. You wished your cat or kid were as obedient. No sound offered so much reassurance that life was good. Rich people would gather at cocktail parties and compare notes. Those in far western Massachusetts might boast that they could now get Boston stations, while those in sober Waco, Texas, would brag that on a clear day they could even bring evil and inebriated Houston into their dry and righteous living rooms. It was something new for Texans to crow about.

But only with the application of the coaxial cable came the possibility of consistently transmitting audio and visual images with crystalline clarity, through electrical wires, into your home. There was still an antenna, but it was so large, so powerful, and so sophisticated—and its signals so organized through the cable system—that you didn't need to worry about it. In fact, you never saw it. You had no idea where it was, and your relationship with it was on a relaxing, "need-to-know" basis. Only when your TV (or modem) lost its signal and went dark did you realize the antenna (or satellite) was even present somewhere (or absent, as it were, until your cable company got its signal straight). Your service provider asked for your patience; you could barely bring yourself to give it. You still can't. And no one is ever there, it seems, to remind you of the bad old days of snowy reception and rabbit ears. No one speaks up to tell you of how lucky you are to have cable—if indeed you still have it, for more and more consumers are turning to wireless, making cable a relic of the past. And of course, most Americans under thirty are too young to remember the bad old days anyhow.

The coaxial cable, with all its blessings, killed the individual antenna, just as broadband killed dial-up for computers. Oh, and optical fiber cables killed coaxial and are now themselves on their way to dusky death thanks to broadband.

THAT WAS THEN, THIS IS NOW: Although rabbit ears are clearly finished for the most part, they are making a small comeback. As viewers have become disenchanted with cable packages—too costly with too many unwanted channels—they are now opting for local stations plus streaming on such outlets as Netflix and Hulu. Things change—except sometimes, when they don't.

HYPOTHETICAL USAGE IN A SENTENCE BY THE OLD AND SETTLED: "Put some extra Reynolds Wrap on those rabbit ears: I want to see if the shoemaker's going to go for the $32,000 question on opera." —Your grandfather, ordering your father around in 1955, as they were watching *The $64,000 Question*

"REALLY BIG SHEW"

THE MOST AWKWARD MAN ON TV

TIMELINE: The legendary *The Ed Sullivan Show*, a.k.a. *The Toast of the Town*, ran on TV for twenty-three years (1948 to 1971).

INSPIRED GUESS BY THE YOUNG AND RESTLESS: Shaq O'Neal's sneakers.

THE ANCIENT TRUTH: This was how Ed Sullivan, the producer and master of ceremonies for the most successful variety show ever put on American television, pronounced "really big show." Sullivan's really big shew began on television in the late 1940s and was first called *The Toast of the Town*. The variety-show format was really a form of old-fashioned vaudeville on the TV screen, which amazed viewers who grew up with vaudeville. Sullivan's show reached the acme of popularity and acclaim in the '50s to the mid-'60s.

Sullivan's variety show featured "acts" that

included jugglers, acrobats, magicians, dancers, and ventriloquists. It also featured "stars," such as Elvis Presley and the Beatles (pronounced slowly by Sullivan as BEEEEET-uls). He was famously persnickety about the moral standards of his show. He made sure Elvis Presley's swiveling groin was never shown on camera (and also endorsed Presley for millions as "a really nice boy," thus easing the panic of American parents who weren't at all sure about the young man whom their daughters swooned to wed and their sons wanted to mimic). He mandated that the Rolling Stones's "Let's Spend the Night Together" be sung as "Let's Spend *Some Time* Together."

Sullivan was a wooden, ungainly man with eyes embedded deep into a forehead topped with thinning brown hair. If speaking had been walking, then he did so in a thick and halting gait. He had all the charisma of a file cabinet but managed to capitalize on it in two ways. He made it his trademark and gladly made it a recurrent source of mockery and self-mockery. And his own deadpan delivery made for a brilliant contrast with the lively acts on his really big shew. It was a weekly production he spent hours on: securing and managing the acts, scheduling them, deciding when they would appear, figuring out how they would be introduced, and so forth. A former entertainment gossip columnist, he became the nation's leading impresario. He was also a star maker; comedians whom he "made," such as George Carlin and Richard Pryor, also became part of the nation's growing late-night talk show culture when, after their stand-up routines on the *Tonight* show, they were invited "back to the couch" for chitchat so that Americans could get to know them better.

The variety show lived a long time on American television. It was a product not only of vaudeville memories but also of a time when there were only three major networks and the generation gap was still small enough that the whole family could sit around on Sunday nights and watch Ed Sullivan introduce everything from Russian ballet to the corniest new comedian.

As it was said at the time, "If Christ's resurrection happened today, Ed Sullivan would give it five minutes on Sunday night." After a stunning solo version of "The Lord's Prayer," Sullivan led the applause and stated, "Let's hear it for the Lord's Prayer."

THAT WAS THEN, THIS IS NOW: Today, if we wish, we can program our own "variety" show, as websites, smartphone apps, YouTube, cable, and streaming offer all the video entertainment we could ever want. Today's millennials, unlike boomer kids, no longer have to watch TV with their elders. To be sure, variety shows might occasionally come back for a PBS special to raise money, and there are aspects of them on talk and talent shows. But for the most part, the old-fashioned variety show lives on today through programs such as *America's Got Talent* as well as late-night talk shows. Ed Sullivan paved the way for comic hosts such as Jay Leno, David Letterman, Jimmy Fallon, and Conan O'Brian, whose programs often feature skits, monologues, musical acts, and more.

HYPOTHETICAL USAGE IN A SENTENCE BY THE OLD AND SETTLED: "Ed Sullivan's *really big shew* must have fit a little too tight last night; he seemed stiffer than ever." —One high school wiseacre newly endowed with a small gift for puns, speaking to another on a Monday morning in November, about 1956

RECORD HOP

WHEN SOCKS
WERE
REQUIRED

TIMELINE: The term, generally synonymous with "sock hop," was popular in the 1950s and early 1960s.

INSPIRED GUESS BY THE YOUNG AND RESTLESS: It must be some sort of Olympic record set for hopping long distances.

THE ANCIENT TRUTH: A record hop was a dance held in the gyms of American high schools during the early period of rock 'n' roll. They began in about 1955. Because high school kids back then tended to wear leather shoes with hard soles, it was necessary for the young and fresh-faced dancers to remove their footwear to protect the gymnasium floor. Thus when they hopped around to the tunes of Elvis Presley or Little Richard or Chuck Berry, they did so in their stocking feet. The guys would wear sport coats (generally no tie) while the girls would wear long, flaring dresses (lots of petticoats). Finally—this was inevitable—a band called Danny and the Juniors recorded a song just for this occasion: 1957's rollicking "At the Hop." Naturally, "At the Hop" became a favorite.

> **Well, you can rock it, you can roll it,**
> **You can slop, and you can stroll it at the hop.**

A record or sock hop was often driven by no more than a portable record player—lots of **45 rpms**—placed near a microphone. But not always: sometimes there was a local DJ spinning those records and increasingly a local band, as rock 'n' roll became more and more mainstream. This was back in the day when some parents, seeing the success of rock 'n' roll stars like Buddy Holly, began to wish they'd given their sons guitar instead of piano lessons.

Record hops often featured a line, formed by each dancer holding onto the hips of the dancer behind him or her. The line would then act as one unit, hopping about the gym floor in a snakelike formation. Sometimes there would be several of these a night, and hops frequently ended on this upbeat and coordinated note. As the 1960s went on, the innocent and chaperoned record hops in bright gyms largely disappeared in favor of drug-fueled rock concerts. By then, it was only the middle school kids who were going to public dances where all the lights were kept on.

THAT WAS THEN, THIS IS NOW: Given the profusion of sneakers and running shoes these days, very few young folks today need to wear socks on the gym floor. So the socks have been taken out of the hop, and few people refer to dances as hops any longer anyhow. And so has the "record" been removed. The availability of music includes digital transmission now, not to mention sound systems of amazing clarity. No phonograph records are required. Even CD players are now antiquated. At school dances today, you'll typically find DJs playing the latest hits in mp3 format, using a laptop or iPod.

In 2010, Artie Singer, one of the writers of "At the Hop," said that Dick Clark would not play the song on *American Bandstand* unless he got half the publishing proceeds. This was apparently a common way of doing business during the early days of rock 'n' roll. But by the later 1950s, the practice of paying disc jockeys to play your records—call "payola"—was frowned upon and even prosecuted.

HYPOTHETICAL USAGE IN A SENTENCE BY THE OLD AND SETTLED:

"You want to go to the record hop tomorrow night, Dottie? I think I can borrow Dad's new DeSoto for wheels." —Jim Hall, asking Dorothy Berry out on a date in 1957

ROAD PICTURES

FROM BALI TO ZANZIBAR

TIMELINE: There were seven "road" motion pictures that ran from 1940 to 1962.

INSPIRED GUESS BY THE YOUNG AND RESTLESS: Digital images stored on smartphones for shared entertainment during long travel.

THE ANCIENT TRUTH: A road picture was one of seven in a series of comic films starring comedian Bob Hope, singer Bing Crosby, and actor-comic Dorothy Lamour. The series ran from 1940 to 1962; an eighth one was planned as late as 1977, but the project ended with the sudden death of Crosby. In their day, the road pictures were quite popular. And it was no wonder, given the tastes of the time. Audiences got Hope's comedy, Crosby's singing, and Lamour's pulchritude, plus the great fun being made of Hollywood action films set in the Far East (intrigue), Africa (safaris), and Alaska (gold rush).

In all, the seven road pictures took viewers on a journey to Singapore, Zanzibar, Morocco, Utopia, Rio, Bali, and Hong Kong. The formula was always the same. Crosby and Hope play a couple of good-natured but irresponsible guys (referred to as "you boys") who seek a holiday from work and look to find introductions to "girls." Prolonged adolescence was a pervasive theme. They have a penchant for offering quick one-liners (especially Hope, who, trying to be a tough guy on the road to Alaska, ordered a "lemonade in a dirty glass"), breaking into crooning melodies (especially Crosby, who sang "Ain't Got a Dime to My Name" on his carefree road to Morocco), and running into a gorgeous woman who blends ample femininity and good sport (almost always Lamour, who emerged as the favorite straight gal in the U.S. of A.; Bud Abbott of **Abbott and Costello** was probably the favorite straight guy). Sometimes the boys are con men, but they always end up more or less reformed, and they often rout some bad guys who are much bigger crooks than they are. The end of the raucous road is always a happy one.

One of the boys in the road pictures (generally Crosby) ends up with Lamour. There are a lot of miscommunications about who loves whom. Hope and Crosby are given such character names as "Fearless," "Turkey," "Scat," and "Hot Lips."

THAT WAS THEN, THIS IS NOW: Some aspects of the road pictures endure today. Although the pictures' versions of Bali and Zanzibar were shot on a Hollywood back lot, there is still an audience interested in exotic locales. And the character of the "man boy" (such as Phil on

ABC's *Modern Family* and Kevin on the American version of *The Office* on NBC) continues to endure. But other aspects of the road pictures seem outdated, such as Hope's and Crosby's over-the-top slapstick and Crosby's sappy crooning. This is a more understated age than the mid-century epoch in which the road pictures were popular. The ersatz Hollywood versions of Rio and Hong Kong would also carry much less appeal at a time when you can visit those places virtually on your laptop or hop a cheap flight you found on the Internet. Going on the road—and getting into the air—is a lot easier than it used to be.

HYPOTHETICAL USAGE IN A SENTENCE BY THE OLD AND SETTLED:

"I first met your beautiful grandmother on a passenger train to Walla Walla. It was just like a road picture—except that your grandmother was more lovely than Lamour and I wasn't as funny as Hope." —Lamar Canafax, Bellingham, Washington, speaking to his grandchildren in 1950

RUNNING BOARD

SHOWING OFF YOUR RACCOON COAT

TIMELINE: Automobile running boards had their heyday during the days of what we would call "vintage cars."

INSPIRED GUESS BY TODAY'S YOUNG AND RESTLESS: A motorized skateboard.

THE ANCIENT TRUTH: The running board was a standard piece of equipment on automobiles during the first four decades of the twentieth century. These models, which were closer to the horse-drawn carriage from which they evolved than today's models, were built much higher off the ground. A running board was a long metal board that eased your descent from the car to the ground. It was like the steps train conductors and bus drivers use today to make sure the distance between the vehicle and the ground is not so great as to result in slips, falls, sprains, fractures—or lawsuits.

Today's SUVs and some trucks continue to have running boards, but they are no longer standard features on all automobiles. And today's younger people, when they see or use a running board—or "extra step"—have no idea of what role running boards played when they were a new and central feature of the American cultural landscape.

Once upon a time in America, running boards were about much more than just standards of safety. They were part of an iconic American image in the Roaring Twenties. They were used on large, eight-cylinder, bulletproof automobiles as a platform for the rum-running gangsters created by Prohibition. It was not every plug-ugly who could stand secure on a running board at fifty miles an hour while still managing to fire a machine gun at the opposition gang. It was a daredevil thing to do. Hollywood films about gangsters couldn't resist the image and often filmed it on back lots. Members of the outfit tended to be deficient in most of the virtues, but they generally did well with courage (or is it bravado?). When running boards were standard equipment, they were supposed to facilitate steps down and steps up. They were not meant to be a narrow standing area for tommy gun practice on human targets. But that is what the gangs made them. Therefore utility and messaging (with bullets) were ingeniously blended. Crooks at their best are creative; at their worst, merely crooked.

The iconic American running board was not just for gun-toting gangsters. Especially during the 1920s, it was also fashionable to stand on the running board for fun, especially on the way to school or to football games. "Hop on!" was the watchword, and before long, the driver had ten passengers: three in the front, three in the back, and *four* on the running boards! At twenty miles per hour, it was all pretty safe. In those days before air-conditioning, the windows were open to the summer air, thus there was a handy place to hold on to—the inside of the car itself—while you had your delightful running board lift.

THAT WAS THEN, THIS IS NOW: Running boards remain as necessary safety features on recreational vehicles and vans and as fashion statements on other cars and trucks. But the running board is no longer a standard feature, nor is it an accoutrement for any iconic images of American life. For today's millennials, a running board—if they know the term—is just a running board. On the other hand, young people still stand on skateboards to say something about themselves. And of course, if they are looking for a "platform" to stand and assert themselves on, there is always Facebook.

HYPOTHETICAL USAGE IN A SENTENCE BY THE OLD AND SETTLED: "As soon as Jed Daniels exceeds thirty miles an hour, I want you off that running board." —A father giving stern instructions to his son, around 1925

SHE WEARS THE PANTS IN THE FAMILY

BEFORE FEMINISM

TIMELINE: The origin of this expression is unknown, but it was primarily used throughout the 1950s and '60s to describe the power struggle between husbands and wives. By the 1970s, women wearing trousers became fairly common, and the phrase started to lose a lot of its meaning and its sting.

INSPIRED GUESSES BY TODAY'S YOUNG AND FOOLISH: A woman who insists that the most expensive pants worn by family members belong to her.

THE ANCIENT TRUTH: "She wears the pants in the family" was a phrase used derisively, mostly by men, to refer to wives who took financial power in a nuclear family. Thus a woman who wore the pants in the family controlled its purse strings, overruled her husband about how money was spent, and generally told her husband what to do: how to dress, where to apply for work, when to get home. A woman who wore the pants in the family was generally in possession of a "henpecked" husband, who thus became a poor and put-upon rooster. He did not wear a dress, but everyone thought he might as well.

The current generation of young people is so accustomed to people of both genders wearing trousers that they can scarcely imagine an astonishing fact: even fifty years ago, it was not okay. This is a struggle with a long and bitter history. Coal-mining women in Britain in the nineteenth century scandalized owners and fellow workers alike by wearing pants to ward off coal dust, and they were made to wear dresses over them upon pain of being fired. Movie stars such as Marlene Dietrich and Katharine Hepburn wore trousers casually and daringly in the 1940s and proved to housewives and clerks in the Midwest that they were laws unto themselves. Yet women wearing trousers was a practice rarely met with smiles.

Traditionally, long dresses (and, for that matter, corsets and petticoats) were worn not only to cover up women's limbs, thus desexualizing them into a proper form of "modesty," but also to emphasize that their proper role was in the home—and not to leave it to labor in offices or factories. But during both world wars, women did mechanical war work while the men fought overseas. They demanded they be given leave to dress appropriately. After World War II, they were expected to go back to the kitchen and don petticoats and decorous high heels to cook with gleaming white stoves. Yet many women who had experienced successful (if temporary) careers outside of the home were unsatisfied. In the 1950s, only four out of ten women worked. But 1950s women might dare to wear "pedal pushers" or "clam diggers" around the house on Saturday if they were sure no one would ring the doorbell. By 1975, pantsuits were becoming commonplace.

By 1980, many guests would *expect* to find their hostesses wearing jeans. By 1990, it was designer *ripped* jeans.

THAT WAS THEN, THIS IS NOW: "She wears the pants in the family" is now an anachronistic expression. Given the ubiquity of trousers across both genders today, the phrase means nothing: *everyone*, whether powerful or powerless, wears pants in the family now. This doesn't mean, though, that power struggles between husbands and wives are over. They remain all too common in conflicts over money and status, issues of "high maintenance," and various types of cultural and temperamental incompatibility. Husbands and wives with equal power would seem to be rare. More likely, it is one or the other who is more powerful, although nowadays it is increasingly possible that it is the wife. But they all wear pants.

HYPOTHETICAL USAGE IN A SENTENCE BY THE OLD AND SETTLED: "Alma always insisted that she wear the pants in the family, but I at least was allowed to make a few big decisions, such as whether or not I liked the United Nations." —Whittaker Shockley, in 1946

SINGING TELEGRAM

BEFORE APPS
WERE
EVERYWHERE

TIMELINE: The first singing telegram was delivered in 1933, but demand for telegrams in general was vastly reduced due to home telephones and the decreasing costs of long-distance calls.

INSPIRED GUESS BY TODAY'S YOUNG AND RESTLESS: A phone app that will give you text messages set to music.

THE ANCIENT TRUTH: Singing telegrams date back long before smartphones, but it was another type of phone—a regular dial-up telephone—that put the singing telegram out of business. The first singing telegram occurred in the early 1930s when an employee of Western Union, the nation's biggest telegram company, got the idea of having a telegram operator sing a message (over the phone) to the then-famous singer Rudy Vallée. At first, everyone snickered at Western Union, but soon enough, the amusing idea caught on. In the '30s, the heyday of the singing telegram, the delivery boy might ring your doorbell and sing "Jenny and the kids do say today/Happy birthday to Uncle Ray."

Telegrams in general were the primary way to send messages if you didn't have a phone or couldn't afford long-distance calls. After World War II, the phones had become widely available, and long distance got cheaper by the year. By the 1970s, telegrams themselves had become requested so infrequently that Western Union pulled the singing service. Now fax machines, email, and text messages, not to mention the phone, have put telegrams out of business almost completely. In India, the country's state owned telecom service still sent out five thousand telegrams a day well into the 2000s—but on July 15, 2013, it sent out its last. The service had lost money for the company for too long.

THAT WAS THEN, THIS IS NOW: For all the ways that communications have changed since Rudy Vallée got the first singing telegram over eighty years ago, singing telegrams are not quite gone. Today's millennials may still have an idea of what a singing telegram is. In February 2012, on the Fox comedy show *Glee*, members decided to deliver Valentine's Day well-wishes in the form of love songs. And private firms, mostly in our largest cities, still offer singing telegram services, such as a BabyGram (where the delivery guy is dressed up like a baby) or an Austin Powers or Barbra Streisand telegram delivered by someone imitating these two luminary talents. You can get a message delivered by a belly dancer or (of course) a clown. Even Western Union, still operating as a money order service, offers an online service in which you can get in touch with your cousin Margaret, for instance, via a digitally composed version of a Snoop Dogg song. Finally, telegrams have come back in new form; now it's called texting. As the young and restless might predict, apps for singing text messages can't be far behind. Can you set "lol" to the tune of a Britney Spears song?

If text messages have their own argot—lol (*laugh out loud*, not lots of love, as some think)—then so did telegrams, with their truncated, punchy discourse and elaborate STOPS for periods: ARRIVE DETROIT 12/2 STOP NEED MONEY STOP SELL CHICKEN FARM STOP COUSIN RENNIE. Try singing that to the tune of, say, "You'll Never Walk Alone" or "Climb Every Mountain."

HYPOTHETICAL USAGE IN A SENTENCE BY THE OLD AND SETTLED:

"Let's send Uncle Arlis one of those new singing telegrams for his seventieth birthday; he'll just hate it." —Your grandmother speaking about a certain mean and miserly relative, in 1936

SLIDE RULE

WHEN ALIGNMENT WAS EVERYTHING

TIMELINE: It was invented in the 1600s and reached its peak of American popularity after World War II when the college-age population, including veterans, began to burgeon. By the mid-1970s, electronic calculators had made the slide rule obsolete.

INSPIRED GUESS BY TODAY'S YOUNG AND RESTLESS: Probably a playground rule, such as "Don't go down head first unless you wear a helmet."

THE ANCIENT TRUTH: A slide rule was what people used to make complex mathematical calculations before the present days of electronic calculators and computers. Actually, the slide rule, developed separately in the 1620s by Edmund Gunter in Oxford and Edmund Wingate in Paris, *was* a computer, but by today's lights, it didn't look like one. Most slide rules looked like elaborate rulers with various sliding scales attached, but you could also find them in cylindrical or wheel form. In the mid-twentieth century, they often fit into a narrow leather belt holster, which kept the slide rule (which might be ten or twenty inches long) snuggly fitted away when not in use.

The slide rule was a quick and handy way to multiply and divide larger numbers and to calculate the various functions of the triangle. Its existence is based on what they *don't* tell children who watch *Sesame Street* and see episodes sponsored by the number eight: that numbers are not stand-alone but have complex relationships to other numbers, which in turn have complex relationships to yet more numbers…well, you get the idea. The number eight is between seven and nine. Four eights make thirty-two. If you "cube" eight (8×8×8), you'll get 512. And this is just the start of things. Likewise, angles in a triangle have intricate relationships. An angle in a triangle has implications for the line across from it and the line under it. These are called functions, as anyone who has ever (barely) passed trigonometry may recall—for whom "sine" was never fine.

A slide rule allowed you to line up the various sliding scales in certain ways in order to find—rapidly—the answers to these calculations. You could multiply, divide, find angular functions, cube, square, and much more: all sorts of things were possible with this sliding little stick. There was only one problem: you had to know how to use one, and it wasn't easy to learn. You couldn't just slide by.

THAT WAS THEN, THIS IS NOW: The slide rule was first conquered by the stand-alone electronic calculator, and now the latter has become much more rare thanks to computers and even smartphones that can perform complex calculations. The slide rule is to all this

Just as doctors carry stethoscopes, preachers carry Bibles, and lawyers tote briefcases, so once upon a time, during the quarter century after World War II, did engineers and scientists and mathematicians (geeks all, to their detractors) carry slide rules, which were conspicuous in their carrying belts even before they were drawn out to do their business.

innovation what the quill pen was to ballpoint. While the slide rule did allow its users to see numbers in their glorious relationships to each other—something a digital calculator does not show—don't head into a contemporary math or science class with one. Young students will not know what it is. They will become bewildered. They will think you very offbeat. They may worry that you will even pummel them with the thing. A slide rule is against the rules. It is, today, numerical backsliding.

HYPOTHETICAL USAGE IN A SENTENCE BY THE OLD AND SETTLED:
"If you don't put that slide rule away and come to bed with me, I'm going to start using it to swat flies." —Mrs. Buckalew, speaking to Dr. Buckalew, astronomer, in 1955

"'T'AINT FUNNY, MCGEE!"

THE CLOSET FROM HELL

TIMELINE: *Fibber McGee and Molly* was on the radio for twenty-four years, from 1935 to 1959.

INSPIRED GUESS BY TODAY'S YOUNG AND RESTLESS: The final verdict from the judges when contestant Eddie McGee is booted off *America's Got Talent*.

THE ANCIENT TRUTH: "'T'aint funny, McGee" was a catchphrase known to virtually every living American from the mid-1930s to the early 1960s. It was the put-down line often delivered on national radio by a character named Molly McGee of 79 Wistful Vista (city or town unknown) to her husband, Fibber.

The McGees were America's most popular radio couple. They were played by Jim and Marian Jordan, sweethearts in the 1910s in Peoria, Illinois. They came from working-class Catholic families, but they had a gift for comedy and repartee and

Fibber said the first name he was supposed to have, *Fimmer,* was muddled because the no doubt well-meaning physician had a head cold, but then Fibber stated lots of things, little of which could be relied upon. It likely that he was *fibbing* about this, as about most things.

the determination to make it pay. In time, they migrated to Chicago, where they made it big on the radio. Their first big venture was a weekly sitcom called *Smackout*, about a general store manager who told customers he was "smack out" even when he had plenty of supplies on hand. And then the Johnson Wax Company agreed to sponsor them nationally in the mid-1930s with their immortal *Fibber McGee and Molly*. Every week, millions of listeners, plus an in-studio live audience, came into the McGee household, where Fibber never held down a job, always concocted schemes (drilling for oil in the backyard), constantly gushed with braggadocio, and spewed the worst puns on the planet. Fibber and Molly had "common American" demeanor, right down to the famous overstuffed hall closet that exploded in avalanche when opened by the unsuspecting burglar or doctor on a house call. They also had a lot of friends and acquaintances in their hilarious universe, including the following:

- *Throckmorton P. Gildersleeve, who gave both pumped-up ostentation and mild chicanery an epic meaning during the Depression years*
- *The Old-Timer, whose real name was never revealed and who misunderstood everything but had diamond-hard convictions that he was always correct*

> ❧ *Tini, a little girl (played by Marian) whose balderdash and zany discourse, in tweety voice, was both hilarious to the audience and infuriating to McGee*
>
> ❧ *Wallace Wimple, the browbeaten hubby whose wife **wore the pants** in the family and whose name may have given rise to the term "wimp" (or was it the other way around?)*

This mélange of characters blended together in plots about life's penny-ante quarrels over toothaches, holidays, burglars, leaf raking, illness, and much more. The back-and-forth on the show was akin to that of the screwball comedies coming out of Hollywood—the rapid-fire quibbles such as McGee's remark that he wouldn't let Dr. Gildersleeve, the dentist, "fill a tooth in my pocket comb." Gildersleeve retaliated by flirting with Molly and giving McGee "mustard gas," appropriate (he opined) for a "ham."

It was McGee's fate to tell awful jokes, avoid work, and be reined in by the far more sensible Molly, though in real life it was Marian Jordan who had the drinking problem while Jim outlived her by twenty-seven years. A TV network tried to adapt Fibber and Molly to the small screen with different actors, but the essence of the show was radio and voice, not television and visuals. Their humor was aural, not like the later physical humor of another famous down-state Illinois comedian, Dick Van Dyke. But even after television had become America's leading source of entertainment—in the late 1950s—the Fibber and Molly radio show remained fairly popular. Even in the age of *I Love Lucy* and *The Honeymooners*, millions didn't want to lose their favorite radio couple. For them, Fibber's groaning puns were hard to give up.

THAT WAS THEN, THIS IS NOW: What would the current young and restless make of *Fibber McGee and Molly*? They would recognize the trope of characters who are funny to others but not to themselves—those, like George Costanza and Cosmo Kramer on *Seinfeld*, who cannot see how absurd they are. The self-absorption of the *Seinfeld* characters has nothing on old McGee. And then Fibber and Molly are also prototypes for another sitcom device: the bickering couples. Any television visit to *Friends* (1994–2004) after season seven will find the nit-picking Monica Geller and the acid Chandler Bing, recently married and already squabbling to hilarious effect. Fibber and Molly had nothing on Monica and Chandler.

HYPOTHETICAL USAGE IN A SENTENCE BY THE OLD AND SETTLED: "'T'aint funny, McGee!" —Your great-grandmother, telling your grandfather that his latest knock-knock joke lacks even a scintilla of humor, in 1939

TELEPHONE NOOK

 # 64

WHEN PHONES WERE FURNITURE

TIMELINE: The phone nook was popular during the days when virtually every American home had only one telephone (1900–1950), which held central pride of place as the family's precious audio lifeline to the outside world.

INSPIRED GUESS BY TODAY'S YOUNG AND RESTLESS: A distraction from the real function of cell phones, which is to send text messages.

THE ANCIENT TRUTH: A phone nook was a little shelf in the home designed specifically to hold the family telephone and perhaps the phone book. A typical telephone nook, often built into a hallway wall, was about a foot high from top to bottom. Beneath the shelf was a flat, attached, semiclosed rectangular area that was flush with the wall and often featured an ornate design. The phone nook wasn't just functional; it was a formal piece of

furniture and ultimately served as a barrier between good taste and the vulgarity of the "device."

From 1920 to 1950, it wasn't polite to talk on the phone in the living room or parlor. The phone was a convenient but strictly regulated device so that it might not intrude upon the family or the privacy of the speaker. It was thought polite for the conversationalist to shut the door during a phone call so as not to disturb others. It was also understood that telephones were not, and never would be, portable. The idea of walking through the house while chatting on the telephone and disturbing everyone's peace and quiet would have been deemed indecent. If pious Americans gave the family Bible a privileged place in the home, it gave the telephone that privilege more grudgingly and secretively.

From about 1900 to 1920, telephones had bases that were too small to house the ringer, so the ringer was stored in the bottom or second part of the nook. There it was hidden, though a tacky wire often came snaking out of the apertures and plugged into the wall. The ringer was screwed to the back of the wood to make sure it was able to steady itself while ringing. Some early phone users were chagrined already that the dignified silence of the household had to be disturbed by the telephone bell. Though they suspected it was the devil's own instrument, they gave in to the temptation of convenience and tried to domesticate it with the ornate nook. For some of them, however, there might well have been a different message: "We not only have a phone, but also a decorated place for it just to make sure you notice our status."

Later phones had bases large enough to house the ringer, so the bottom half of the nook was empty and thus totally free to display its, by now, wireless beauty. By the '40s, it had become such a standard feature of complementary beauty that builders often retained it. Some residents back then still thought that a phone without a nook was almost as bad as renting out the upstairs to a nudist colony.

But then came late 1950s American prosperity, and with it the acquisition of second phones. With the introduction in 1959 of the princess phone—a colorful compact bedroom phone (red, white, yellow, blue, etc.) meant to look good and not just work well—and the post–World War II economic boom, the days of the single-phone house were numbered. By 1960, new homes with phone nooks were in the past, and even older homes, with phones more scattered around the premises, began to use them to support old vases or potted plants, not ancient black telephones.

THAT WAS THEN, THIS IS NOW: Today, when approximately 88 percent of Americans own a portable cell phone and nearly half own smartphones, there is no need for a phone nook in the home. A permanent "pride of place" for the phone is an outmoded and irrelevant idea. Perhaps that's not altogether good; if we had a devoted place for our phones, we wouldn't have to search so frantically for them in the morning. Meanwhile, phone etiquette, so strict during those halcyon pre–cell phone days, is ever-evolving but unregulated. How many obnoxious cell phone conversations have you been privy to in an airport or restaurant lately? You can't tell these loquacious folks to head to the hall and shut the door, please.

HYPOTHETICAL USAGE IN A SENTENCE BY THE OLD AND SETTLED: "Should we put the nook on the east or west wall of the downstairs corridor?" —Your great-grandfather, speaking to the carpenters, in about 1926

65

T FORMATION

THRILLING THE NATION

TIMELINE: It was one of football's earliest offensive schemes, dating to the late nineteenth century. It was later adapted and reached its peak in the 1940s and '50s.

INSPIRED GUESS BY TODAY'S YOUNG AND RESTLESS: A spray used for testosterone-deficient males after they've ordered it from late-night TV ads.

THE ANCIENT TRUTH: The T formation was one of the greatest strategic innovations in the history of American football. Invented in 1882 by Yale's football innovator, Walter Camp, it became discredited for a while until coaches figured out how to blend it with that increasingly popular and powerful weapon known as the forward pass (now just called a pass). It is credited with helping the 1940 Chicago Bears defeat the Washington Redskins 73–0 in the championship game, leading to a line in the Bears' fight song:

"We remember how you thrilled the nation/With your T formation." In the 1950s, the Oklahoma Sooners won forty-seven games in a row using the T. Now it has largely disappeared from professional football.

Football strategies usually depend upon unpredictability: the fact that one team cannot know what the other team will do. This need for sudden surprise explains why the upgraded T formation—with seven players, mostly blockers, lined up horizontally across the top of the T and four players, mostly running backs, lined up vertically at the T's bottom—became so popular in the 1930s, once it was upgraded from the rather crude formation designed by Walter Camp fifty years earlier. This "T 2.0" kept opponents off balance and became all the rage.

The central fact of T 2.0 was that the ball was snapped directly to the quarterback under the center. T formation plays developed quickly and kept the opposition hesitant and guessing because there were so many different things the quarterback could do once the center had delivered the ball to him: hand off to one of the three running backs, keep the ball and run with it himself, pass to one of the ends at the top of the T, pretend to hand off to one of the running backs but actually pass the ball, and so on. Running backs could even hand off, or pass, the ball to one another.

But there was still a flaw in T 2.0: for all its virtues, there are other formations that are even *better* adapted to the forward pass. T 2.0 kept too many potential pass catchers behind the line of scrimmage at the outset of the play. It depended upon ends who could block rather than ends who could catch. Nowadays, these "ends" are called "wide receivers."

The T is adapted to a running game—where it is very smart indeed—but it's much less useful for passing. In the 1960s, Darrell Royal, the successful coach at the University of Texas, remarked that he didn't believe in a lot of passing because if you passed, three things could happen, and two of them (an incompletion or an interception) were bad. Royal believed that football was about running the ball: three yards and a cloud of dust. But few coaches follow Mr. Royal's philosophy any longer.

> When Sid Luckman, the Chicago Bears quarterback in the '30s and '40s, began to operate the T, he discovered that in terms of hand-offs, passes, places to run, adjustments, and so forth, the T could generate nearly one hundred variants. Football should be called chess with brutes. Maybe Bobby Fischer would have nothing on Sid Luckman.

In our era, pass plays are now much more likely to succeed, and with longer ones, the opportunity for yardage gains outweighs the risk. Today's pro passers are remarkably accurate. They have almost bionic arms for getting the ball down the field. Offenses are like machines, sometimes to the point where the quarterback will know where fleet pass receivers are at all times and can get the ball to them within two seconds of the snap from center. Even so, it requires lots of receivers downfield, and this requirement has spelled the end for the classical T. But perhaps some genius out there is devising a "T 3.0"!

THAT WAS THEN, THIS IS NOW: The T is not coming back. In today's game, which is dominated by the pass, adding two extra running backs is a waste and counterproductive. Only a team that wishes, all too predictably, to run the ball nearly all the time would go with the

T; perhaps a few high school teams, but there are no such squads on the professional gridiron today. Nonetheless, the T's legacy made the quarterback the central player on offense. Without it, Aaron Rodgers and Drew Brees would not be where they are today.

HYPOTHETICAL USAGE IN A SENTENCE BY THE OLD AND SETTLED:

"The only T formation I'm interested in is trigonometry." —Your great-grandfather, chastising your grandfather, who was captain of the football team but failing math, in 1940

TIRED BLOOD

GET UP AND GO!

TIMELINE: Geritol has been on the market since 1950. Its peak of popularity was in the 1950s and '60s.

INSPIRED GUESS BY TODAY'S YOUNG AND RESTLESS: A retro rock band.

THE ANCIENT TRUTH: Tired blood was the commercial name for iron-deficiency anemia, the malady mentioned over and over again by the makers of Geritol, a once alcohol-based, iron-rich tonic that was supposed to treat such a problem. Geritol was at its most popular in the 1950s and '60s, when the brand sponsored the popular quiz show *Twenty One* and then *The Lawrence Welk Show*, Ted Mack's ***The Original Amateur Hour***, and *What's My Line?* The name Geritol brings to mind "geriatric," and indeed the product was primarily marketed toward the elderly. On occasion, it featured young people who said they took Geritol.

In 1973, its manufacturers got into trouble with federal investigators. Iron-deficiency anemia is a specific medical condition that can be relieved by getting more iron into the bloodstream. But there are all sorts of reasons for fatigue, especially among the elderly. As a result, many folks who did not suffer from iron-deficiency anemia took the elixir anyhow. Too *much* iron can indirectly cause other medical problems, including arthritis, oversensitivity to sunlight, and liver disease. While the makers of Geritol always insisted that their potential consumers should see their doctors, this advice was quickly swamped by claims that, in just twenty-four hours, they could "feel stronger fast" with just a couple of good swigs of Geritol. In 1965, the Food and Drug Administration fined the company over $800,000 ($4.2 million today) for sketchy advertising.

As the great (now septuagenarian) writer Joan Didion has said about aging in her 2011 memoir *Blue Nights*, there is a "blue night" in autumn between the afternoon sun and the enveloping dark. Old people know that blue night in their own descent and seem powerless to arrest it. But to fight the encroaching flabbiness of tissue, the languor of soft decline—to battle the blue night—with *iron*: what could be more appealing? Iron is strong and firm! It is young! It is rigorous and vigorous! One has the impression of an iron filament coursing through one's veins and turning the blood itself into a vessel of churning if rigid vitality. The tired man becomes the iron man. Or perhaps the iron will turn the blood from a weak, bleached-out red into a strong, ruddy red, as almost surely it was when the elderly were just twenty-five years old. Whatever the medical merits of Geritol, its advertising ingenuity is hard to deny.

THAT WAS THEN, THIS IS NOW: Geritol remains available, but its heyday has passed. Consumers have alternative ways to pep up, such as an improved diet, exercise, prescription drugs, herbal remedies, and energy drinks like Red Bull. In addition, today's older people, an increasingly large share of the population, are better educated than their predecessors and have become more consumer-savvy. Prompted by the AARP and other wellness organizations, they think of themselves as a tribe apart, with their own special needs for service and information and means of obtaining them. Today's better-educated older people are aware that the gradual loss of "get up and go" is a more complicated matter, concerning genetics, lifestyle, sleep patterns, and more.

> For all the antiquity of the old Geritol commercials, with their turning "tired blood" into one of the most familiar terms in the America of fifty years ago, human beings in the November of life remain attracted to the quick fix. Yesterday, old people took Geritol; today, they drink Red Bull.

HYPOTHETICAL USAGE IN A SENTENCE BY THE OLD AND SETTLED:

"Don't bug me tonight; I have tired blood." —Your grandfather, trying to get someone to actually *volunteer* to take out the garbage for once

"UM, THAT RIGHT, KEMOSABE"

DOMESTICATING THE FERAL WEST

TIMELINE: *The Lone Ranger* began on the radio in 1933 and has gone through various incarnations as a TV show, an animated cartoon series, and several films.

INSPIRED GUESS BY TODAY'S YOUNG AND RESTLESS: A distant ancestor of Bart Simpson's "Cowabunga, dude."

THE ANCIENT TRUTH: Though it's not entirely clear what "Kemosabe" means, the most common interpretation is "trusty scout" or "trusty friend." The phrase originated on the radio program *The Lone Ranger*, used by the Potawatomi Indian Tonto when he addressed a masked white man named John Reid, who came to be known to millions as the Lone Ranger. On both radio and television, these two fictional characters inspired three generations of youngsters (from the early 1930s to the late '50s) to do right and eat Cheerios, which also happened to be the sponsor of the thirty-minute episodes, all of which were rooted in "those thrilling days of yesteryear" when there was a struggle to bring "law and order to the early West."

The concept was a 1933 creation of Fran Striker and George Trendle, who worked out of a Detroit radio station. They borrowed the moniker "Kemosabe" from a camp in northern Michigan. The Lone Ranger—highly skilled at shooting, horse riding, and fisticuffs—was a former Texas Ranger who was the sole survivor of a sadistic attack led by an outlaw gang. Tonto nursed Reid to recovery. Reid's brother was not so lucky, and so Reid set out to avenge his brother's death, donning a mask fashioned from his slain brother's vest. He made sure that he was never without his mask or friend as he and Tonto fought to bring some semblance of order to those wild, olden times. Soon the Lone Ranger acquired a dashing white stallion named Silver, which he urged on his way with a hearty "hi-yo!"

In the early radio days of *The Lone Ranger,* the producers used classical music for background and transition, not necessarily to promote erudition but because the music was in the public domain and therefore free. Later they bought, on the cheap, some boilerplate music from Republic Pictures cowboy serials and used that. Nonetheless, they never gave up using as the major theme music Rossini's "March of the Swiss Soldiers" from his *William Tell Overture.*

The show carried its share of cultural significance. It tacitly taught the kiddies values, such as a sense of duty, honor, and no shortage of manifest destiny. Among less transcendent rules were these: never become captured by bad guys; never use your silver bullets carelessly;

and never forget that while it's gratifying to defeat bad guys, it's not just about you but also about the development of the Western United States.

THAT WAS THEN, THIS IS NOW: It's clear that *The Lone Ranger* has enduring pop culture power, as the 2013 film with Johnny Depp and Armie Hammer demonstrates. The reboot received negative reviews for being too long and too over-the-top. It tries to be grittily realistic, as is the convention with today's Westerns, so it included a brothel and some railroad corporate chicanery and features Depp, who says he's partly Native American, speaking some Comanche. The film's merits or demerits aside, the Lone Ranger is likely to remain a compelling myth that will reemerge from time to time in film. That's because it's a story of changed American identity: the transformation of a man from unmasked to masked and the emergence of a new man working off his grief as an agent of justice. Acquiring fresh beginnings is hardly an unfamiliar experience to Americans. A 2008 Pew study found that 44 percent of us have switched religious faiths at least once. If John Reid were living today as a typical American, he might well have gone from Presbyterian to transcendental meditation, and on grounds far less traumatic than the death of a brother by outlaw bullets.

HYPOTHETICAL USAGE IN A SENTENCE BY THE OLD AND SETTLED: "Um, that right, Kemosabe." —George Fenton, fifty, speaking to his wife Clara, who reminds him that their son's summer camp, Camp Weni-ha-ha, is coming up on the left, in July 1954

#68 VOLKSWAGEN JOKES

HOW MANY ELEPHANTS?

TIMELINE: These gags were popular in the late 1950s and into the '60s, when Volkswagens were the runts of the American road.

INSPIRED GUESS BY TODAY'S YOUNG AND RESTLESS: Jokes about Volkswagens, but why wouldn't people be joking about SUVs instead?

THE ANCIENT TRUTH: Volkswagen jokes made irreverent fun of the German-made Volkswagen Beetles when they were by far the newest and oddest car on the American highway. The heyday of VW jokes and riddles was the 1960s, which to today's millennials is ancient history. But half a century ago, jokes about the Volkswagen Beetle's quirky design were wildly popular.

- *How do you get two elephants into a Volkswagen? You put one in the front and one in the back.*

- *How do you get four elephants into a Volkswagen? You put two in the front and two in the back.*
- *How do you get six elephants into a Volkswagen? You put two in the front, two in the back, one in the trunk, and one in the glove compartment.*
- *How are an elephant and a Volkswagen alike? They both have trunks in the front.*

After World War II, Americans encouraged the revival of the "Volks" because they wanted a prosperous West Germany as a buffer against the Soviet Union. By the 1960s, imported VW Beetles had a discernible market share in the United States auto market. But those who bought a Beetle weren't just buying a car. They were buying into a *movement*—and it's from that movement that VW jokes arose.

If you purchased a Beetle, you were more than just an "early adopter." You were in implicit but good-natured rebellion against the American convention of big American gas hogs, flashy and swept-winged. The point of the jokes was to think small instead of big, and European, not American. You had proudly committed yourself to the boxy, humpbacked Beetle, with its air-cooled engine in the back, split rear windows, pressurized windshield washers that were hooked up to the overinflated spare tire, and hard-to-find and hard-to-attach seat belts ("Hitler's revenge," they were called). If American eight-cylinder cars could do a hundred miles per hour, the Beetle topped out at seventy or so. But—and this is one of the first things Beetle owners would tell you—it got thirty-six miles on one gallon of gas and (with its engine weight concentrated over the rear tires) provided better traction on frozen roads. From the Beetle's strange shape to its survival on the road, there was something comic, even triumphant, about the VW.

VW drivers liked the idea of being witty enough to paint their Beetle in psychedelic colors. (You'd never do that to a Chrysler Imperial—its delusions of Detroit grandeur would be harmed beyond repair.) You could be a little countercultural, not by protesting in the streets, but by deciding how you'd like to use your pocketbook. You loved those Beetles jokes; you yourself told them, maybe even as a form of boasting about how clever you were as a consumer.

> The Volkswagen was, in the Germany from which it came, the "people's car." In the late 1930s, Hitler wanted mass production of them for the denizens of the Third Reich: a vehicle that could accommodate two adults and three children (in the mind of Der Führer, future goose-steppers and Aryan housekeepers), do up to sixty-two miles per hour, and be paid for in monthly installments. Because of the war and its privations, Germans were never able to produce the car other than in the form of prototypes used by high Nazi officials alone.

THAT WAS THEN, THIS IS NOW: The whole basis of Volkswagen Beetles jokes was the contrast between the gas eaters of the '50s and '60s on America's new interstate highways and the reliable efficiency of the dwarfish Volkswagen. By the 1970s, when Japanese cars began to make significant inroads into American sales, smaller cars became the norm, and the Volks jokes went the way of the Packard, Hudson, and DeSoto. Meanwhile, the original Beetles ideal—that small is beautiful—has triumphed with a vengeance. Think laptops, tablets, and smartphones.

HYPOTHETICAL USAGE IN A SENTENCE BY THE OLD AND SETTLED:

"How do you get seven elephants into a Volkswagen? Come on! Everyone knows you can't get seven elephants into a Volkswagen!" —Bob Wilson, then seventeen, in 1964…now sixty-seven and driving an SUV

#69 WATERGATE

EXPLETIVE DELETED

TIMELINE: The infamous burglary at the Watergate Building occurred in June 1972, and the ensuing Watergate scandal began in earnest in January 1973.

INSPIRED GUESS BY TODAY'S YOUNG AND RESTLESS: An old scandal the Clintons were mixed up in.

THE ANCIENT TRUTH: The Watergate, originally named for its terraced steps that lead down to the Potomac River, is a building in Washington, DC, that unwittingly inspired the most destructive political scandal in American history. One night in June 1972, burglars were caught rifling through the Democratic National Committee headquarters in the Watergate office complex. After the fall elections, the break-in was traced definitively to President Richard Nixon's White House. At that point, Watergate became more than a political scandal—it became a national obsession. Kiddies born in the mid-'60s (now nearly fifty) recall their parents talking often about it and may have wondered why there was so much bother about a gate and how it could lead to a jowly grown-up quitting his job on national TV.

No one seems to know for sure why the burglars (from President Nixon's Committee to Re-Elect the President, mockingly given the acronym CREEP by Nixon's foes) broke into the headquarters of the opposing party. Nixon may have feared the Democrats had information about his brother's shady dealings with billionaire Howard Hughes, but there is no credible evidence that Nixon knew anything about the plot in advance. Far more important than motive was that Nixon and his men chose to cover up the burglars' associations with the reelection committee and the White House. The president ordered the FBI not to investigate the matter further. In doing so, he obstructed justice. Had he come clean from the outset, the subsequent scandal—all the investigations into the burglary and other damaging material about everything from Nixon's profanity to his tax records—would never have come out.

But Nixon was a highly partisan, somewhat paranoid figure who had once lost the presidency narrowly, in 1960, and was in terror about losing it again, even though his Democratic opponent, George McGovern, was far too left wing to defeat him. He decided that being honest about what had happened would be more damaging than hiding it. So he began a year's campaign to secret away the truth and divert the public from the whole affair. He asked that American citizens not follow the lead of his hated Democratic opponents—that they not "wallow in Watergate."

But the public could not be diverted. They were inordinately curious about whether Nixon had anything to hide, and of course they were anxious to believe that their president was not, in Nixon's own words, "a crook." By the summer of 1973, they had come to see him as a shifty, spiteful man on the run from the truth.

For President Nixon, the Watergate scandal came from a perfect storm of troubles. He was a secretive, seething man who believed the Eastern Establishment looked down on him because of his poor background and non-elitist degrees. He wanted to get everything down on tape so that he could screw his enemies, write his memoirs, and maybe one day even sell the transcripts. He thought he had a right to do anything to stay in office because only he could keep the country from becoming dangerously weakened by the Vietnam War— and above all, he thought that if a president did something, it was not illegal.

A central part of the ensuing drama resided in the revelation that President Nixon had secretly recorded all conservations held in his Oval Office. There was an extensive court fight about whether or not he would surrender the tapes to law enforcement officers investigating the break-in. He lost that battle, and the defeat meant the end of his presidency. Not only was he revealed as a petty, profane man (the transcripts of the tapes often featured "expletive deleted" to spare the public the extent of Nixon's four-letter words). He was also exposed as someone who had illegally perverted the course of justice. By August 1974, he was about to be impeached by the House of Representatives, after which the Senate would almost certainly have convicted him. He chose to resign ahead of the posse. In doing so, he did not say he had done any-thing wrong—only that he had lost his base of support in the Congress.

THAT WAS THEN, THIS IS NOW: Watergate will live in infamy as the greatest political scandal in United States history and the only one that forced a presidential resignation. Nonetheless, it is not of great moment for today's young, who were after all born up to two decades after Nixon left office. (For further perspective, let us note that a first-year college student today would have also been only two when the Clinton-Lewinsky scandal struck.) Nonetheless, if President Nixon were alive today, he would be pleased, for at last he would have found a generation no longer interested in "wallowing in Watergate."

HYPOTHETICAL USAGE IN A SENTENCE BY THE OLD AND SETTLED: "Let's see now. Was James McCord one of the Watergate burglars or was he in the FBI or CIA?" —Gregory Foulkes, speaking last year to his wife (McCord was all three)

"WE HAD TO DESTROY THE VILLAGE IN ORDER TO SAVE IT"

AMERICA'S WORST PARADOX

TIMELINE: The startling quotation, attributed to a U.S. Army major, appeared in the press in 1968.

INSPIRED GUESS BY TODAY'S YOUNG AND RESTLESS: Something my parents would say when they're redoing the kitchen—again.

THE ANCIENT TRUTH: An Associated Press reporter named Peter Arnett first reported the sentence in early 1968. He claimed it was a revelatory declaration by an anonymous U.S. Army officer, who effectively admitted that the army had to bomb a South Vietnamese village to keep it from falling into the hands of the North Vietnamese, killing innocent civilians at the same time. The statement's veracity was never established and its source never confirmed or identified. But to both critics of the war and to an increasingly frustrated American public, the phrase suggested that the United States in Vietnam had found itself in an impossible predicament. In a war where the loyalty of local people was essential for long-term victory, the United States, in killing the enemy, was only making *new* enemies—out of the very people it was trying to protect from communism!

In the late 1950s, the Soviet Union announced that it would support communists all over the world who were engaged in "wars of national liberation" to defeat their old European colonial masters, such as the French in Indo-China (now Vietnam). This declaration was enough for many American policy makers, who decided that if the Soviets were going to support the communist factions in these wars, the United States should support the *non*communist ones. And these same policy makers were convinced that if one Southeast Asian country (such as Vietnam) went "commie," they all would, and soon Vietnam, Cambodia, Laos, and Thailand (among others) would be under the iron thumb of "Red" China. This prediction was known as the "domino theory."

This was the background for American involvement on the side of the noncommunist South Vietnamese in what was a civil war. The U.S. effort began slowly in the early 1960s, but within six years, it had grown to half a million troops. As the war wound on without any definitive American victory, more and more Americans began to turn against it. The United States had superior weaponry of all sorts compared to the peasant North Vietnamese and their loyal South Vietnamese allies the Viet Cong, yet it could not seem to win the war and, by 1975, had lost it. Perhaps destroying villages in order to save them was a terrible idea, and maybe it epitomized the tragic mistake of original American involvement.

Yet the once-famed paradox is overrated as an explanation for the American failures in Vietnam, which can really be traced not to the disloyalty of villagers but to the inadvisability of becoming involved in a war of attrition. The fundamental facts were that the North Vietnamese communists had a totalitarian government that did not mind risking hundreds of thousands of lives, and it could outlast the patience of an American public eager for clean-cut victory and the resources of an American military that, after all, could not continue to be bogged down forever in the jungles of Vietnam. American war hero General Douglas MacArthur told President Kennedy in 1961 that any president who committed the U.S. to fighting a land war in Southeast Asia ought to have his head examined. But there is no evidence that either President Kennedy, or successor Lyndon Johnson, ever went for psychiatric treatment about their decisions to do just that.

When Richard Nixon became president in 1969, he suspected that the Vietnam War was not cleanly winnable the way Americans had won World War II. But at the same time, it could not be lost, lest American prestige plummet in a dangerous world inhabited by great foes such as the Soviet Union and China. So he sought to get the South Vietnamese to take over the fighting while slowly pulling out Americans. But not long after Nixon resigned, the war was lost in precisely the way he had dreaded. The American exit was panicky, with South Vietnamese loyal to the United States desperately scrambling to get aboard departing American planes.

THAT WAS THEN, THIS IS NOW: The Vietnam paradox means little or nothing to the present generation. Most of them were not yet born during the ignominious American departure from Vietnam. For them, the country itself is just a little Southeast Asian land of scant significance. But there are a couple of ways in which today's millennials would relate to the old conundrum about destroying villages in order to save them. They have lived through their own paradox: "too big to fail," a reference to enormous Wall Street banks whose tentacles are so wrapped around the American economy that taxpayers must bail them out, lest the entire financial foundations fall down about us all. The near-collapse of the financial industry in 2008 to 2009 is the Vietnam of today's younger folks. And today's generation is all too aware of another American war policy failure: Iraq. But while their grandparents had to worry about being drafted for Southeast Asia, Iraq was fought with an all-volunteer army. Millennials need not fear any coerced military service.

HYPOTHETICAL USAGE IN A SENTENCE BY THE OLD AND SETTLED:

"I had to destroy the car in order to save it." —Timothy Dutton, eighteen, speaking sheepishly to his parents in 1971 about an auto accident; the car already had several bad dents, but now the whole body could be replaced with a brand new one

WORLD BOOK

PRIDE ON THE SHELF

TIMELINE: The *World Book Encyclopedia* first appeared in 1917 in eight volumes. Since then, it has come out virtually every year in updated form and claims to be the number-one bestselling print encyclopedia in the world. It now has a significant online presence too.

INSPIRED GUESS BY TODAY'S YOUNG AND RESTLESS: A Google app that links you to all the catalogs of the world's great libraries.

THE ANCIENT TRUTH: First published in 1917, *World Book Encyclopedia* became a major status symbol in the America after 1945, when the United States emerged as the sole major victor of World War II without any damage to the homeland and with a manufacturing dominance that made it far and away the world's leading economy. Americans in their twenties and thirties had put off having children during the war—it was a time to put such hopeful decisions on hold—but they came up with a great "boom" of newborns once the conflict was over. (The kids are now in their fifties and sixties and looking for their Social Security and Medicare.) After sixteen years of Depression and war, enter as on cue, the *World Book* for a new generation of youngsters. In a time of peace and prosperity, what better way to help your new kid get ahead in life than to purchase for them a set of bound encyclopedias?

And what better choice than the Chicago-based *World Book*? If you purchased a set of *World Books*, it was a sign you were really serious about self-improvement and upward mobility, for yourself and your brood.

The volumes were not of equal size: "X, Y, and Z" was smaller as one volume than "C" was as one and a half. You felt smarter already, and you hadn't even opened one of the books. Experts penned the carefully edited articles in simple, brisk, clear prose, paired with illustrations of vivid and colorful lucidity. By the 1950s, one-third of the contents were illustrations, and by the late 1960s, 80 percent of these were in color.

Parents who made the investment were letting their kids know they expected them to do well in school. The *World Book*'s pride of place on the shelf was a great icon of middle-class aspirations. The kids could employ it to brush up on some basic math. They could find supplemental information about the Sea of Japan and wow their geography teachers. They could even paraphrase from the volumes if they were assigned, say, a little term paper on "famous British inventors." The *World Book* implied, by its very existence, an approval of the "empty vessel" notion of ignorance. You were ignorant not because you could not think—you were ignorant because you did not have any facts in your head. In 1961, *World Book* put out an edition in Braille as a public service. It was in nearly 150 volumes. This was a triumphant expression of its devotion to a democracy of learning. Even the blind can learn that Marilyn Monroe's real name was Norma Jean Baker and that Sofia is the capital of Bulgaria and that dry ice is the solid form of carbon dioxide.

THAT WAS THEN, THIS IS NOW: The *World Book* is still alive today, but in a drastically changed format. It lacks the prestige it had between 1945 and 1995, when it seemed every family with a kid bound for a degree in accounting or marketing also had a set of bound *World Books*. A member of the current generation spoke for his peers when, upon spying a set of *World Books* in the library, he shook his head and said, "I can't believe they printed the whole thing out." The real encyclopedia today is called the Internet. Today, *World Book* offers excellent online production values and some arresting formats of information. Its days as a middle-class status symbol are over—it's just one more source of information—and with increasing degrees of American income inequality in a global economy, some economists, such as Paul Krugman, worry that the middle class may be on the wane as well.

Today, one can purchase bound *World Book Encyclopedias* called "spinescape." One can also subscribe to the online version at worldbook.com or access it at the public library. Today's *World Books* come in two different sets: one for school and library, one for family and home. There is also yet another separate set, for younger kids, called *Discovery* encyclopedias; they include entries on such subjects as graphic novels, Harry Potter, Barack Obama, and rap music.

HYPOTHETICAL USAGE IN A SENTENCE BY THE OLD AND SETTLED:

"Vulgar children read *Superman* comics; we demand that our children read *World Books*." —Sister Mary Catherine at Our Lady's Elementary School, 1953

#72 YOUR HIT PARADE

TOP TEN

TIMELINE: The show ran on the radio from 1935 to '55 and on TV from 1950 to '59.

INSPIRED GUESS BY TODAY'S YOUNG AND RESTLESS: A succession of really great bong hits.

THE ANCIENT TRUTH: *Your Hit Parade* was one of America's most popular music shows for nearly a quarter of a century. It began on the radio in the mid-1930s and ended on television in the late 1950s. The essential format was the performance of the ten bestselling songs in the United States in a given week, starting with the least popular and ending with number one. The American Tobacco Company sponsored the show, featuring the **Lucky Strike** Orchestra and dancing cigarette packs (Lucky Strike packages that moved with bare women's legs). Because the same songs might be popular for many weeks, it was necessary, for the sake of variety, to rotate the singers of those tunes on the radio and change the visual backgrounds to their performance on television. The singers featured at some time or another on the show read like a who's who of famous American vocalists, such as Doris Day and Frank Sinatra.

During the earlier days of the show, records played a relatively small role in the tabulation of what songs were popular and what songs were not. The surveys checked out sheet music sales, jukebox selections, dance hall requests, nightclub performances, and, above all, live radio performances. As a result, it was the song, not the singer, which counted. In the mid-1940s, Sinatra, by then a teen heartthrob, got to perform one of his own songs on the show, but this was the first time this had ever happened—and it remained a rare event indeed thereafter.

THAT WAS THEN, THIS IS NOW: There are still bestselling songs, but the format in which *Your Hit Parade* presented them is long gone. The show operated in an era when the song was more important than the performer who had recorded it. Today, the reverse is true. While, just as in the days of *Your Hit Parade*, some songs are better than others and therefore do better than others, it is the individual performance that counts most of all. It is hard to imagine a program where someone from a group of generic singers—someone other than Lady Gaga—will sing "Judas" every week and reach a national audience.

The great array of talented singers hired by *Your Hit Parade* trained themselves to sing "popular" music, not rock 'n' roll. In the mid-1950s, Snooky Lanson tried to cover Elvis Presley's "Hound Dog." But he did not swivel his hips. He had a good-looking, bland face: the sort you'd see on a supporting player in a Hollywood domestic drama of the 1940s. The whole performance, however game, was so ludicrous that the secret was out: *only Elvis could do "Hound Dog."*

HYPOTHETICAL USAGE IN A SENTENCE BY THE OLD AND SETTLED:

"Turn on the TV. I want to see if 'Oh, My Papa!' is still in third place on *Your Hit Parade*." —Your great-grandmother speaking to your grandmother when she was twelve, in about 1954

YOUR MONEY OR YOUR LIFE

#73

AMERICA'S FUNNIEST DILEMMA

TIMELINE: The gag was first performed on the radio in 1948. Although the number of performances is small, it became known as one of Jack Benny's most famous routines.

INSPIRED GUESS BY TODAY'S YOUNG AND RESTLESS: The title of a pioneering reality show.

THE ANCIENT TRUTH: "Your Money or Your Life" is the best-known gag of celebrated comedian Jack Benny, whose national radio show ran from 1932 to 1955. In this scene, first performed in 1948, Benny is walking late at night when a masked mugger holds him up and demands "your money or your life." Benny remains silent. The audience begins to laugh. Silence. It laughs even more. After a virtual pandemonium of such guffaws, the mugger repeats himself with snarls: "Come on! I said your money or your life!" Benny (with a great deal of exasperation): "I'm thinking it over!" At this point, the audience is out of control.

This was vintage Benny, with the impeccable timing of his silence, the persuasive power of his acting (especially that poignant look of exasperation), and the utter ridiculousness of his situation, as though anyone loved money so much he would rather lose his life than give it up. Yet few people under sixty would laugh at this skit today. That's because Benny's comedy was highly contextualized. The contemporary comedian and talk show host Jay Leno can come on the air and tell a battery of jokes. They are made funnier by Leno's great delivery and timing, but the jokes largely are based on popular news stories that require familiarity with the subject matter to be fully understood.

> Comedians have always made trouble pay, and no trouble in life is so great as the inability to mandate what we want to mandate and order what we want to order. This is the elemental humor of the man slipping on the banana peel. Benny took it to a high art form, with the hilarity implicit in the man who so wants to control life that he'd think about surrendering life itself rather than lose his control of it.

This was not the comic method of Benny, who based his comedy on a long-evolved persona, not an immediate headline. Benny spent years developing his persona as a slightly prissy but always stingy and vainglorious control freak. He brought "cheap" to a new outer limit and gave "loss aversion" a hilarious intensity: he'd almost rather lose his life than part with his dough. His friends endlessly needled him about this trait. Every Benny show had at least four or five comic references to his pathological thriftiness. Often whole plots were built around it, as when Benny drives everyone in a department store crazy because he's always looking for a better bargain.

THAT WAS THEN, THIS IS NOW: "In character" comedy is still with us. Jerry Seinfeld was known for his self-absorption and Roseanne Barr for her vulgarity. Steve Carrell's Michael Scott on the American version of *The Office* is funny for his laid-back ineptitude. But stinginess, which Benny developed to a comic art form, is apparently no longer a funny stereotype. That's because thrift, in excess or moderation, is no longer a preoccupying American virtue. While we have just come through the Great Recession and have cut back to catch up on our bills, this is likely temporary. We live in a world of consumption and in an economy where the personal consumer carries the lion's share of responsibility for growth. The old American habit of saving, in a country where so few are prepped well for retirement, is no longer a great virtue and thus no longer, in pathological form, a comic vice. Though we should be wary of today's still-recovering economy, already economists are warning that dangerous new "bubbles" are forming. Today, we spend and invest; we don't save—and don't prefer to die rather than lose the five bucks in our wallet. If a thief stuck us up as he did Benny (today it's called "being mugged"), we'd likely have less cash than even Benny did, who sashayed about before the days of credit cards, and we'd give over the wallet right away and call Visa immediately in order to cancel the card. If only Jack Benny had had this option!

HYPOTHETICAL USAGE IN A SENTENCE BY THE OLD AND SETTLED: "Your money or your life." —Elbert Johnston speaking to his eleven-year-old son Dennis after he returned from the local bakery in 1951 with a loaf of bread, but without the remaining $0.84 in change

#74 THE ZAPRUDER FILM

A TRUE HORROR FILM

TIMELINE: Abraham Zapruder shot the film of John Kennedy's assassination on November 22, 1963.

INSPIRED GUESS BY TODAY'S YOUNG AND RESTLESS: An indie film by a European director.

THE ANCIENT TRUTH: The Zapruder film is the most famous and complete visual account of the Kennedy assassination. It was shot by a Dallas manufacturer of women's clothing, Abraham Zapruder, a Ukrainian American. He took his 8 mm Bell and Howell Camera, along with his receptionist to steady him on one of the concrete pedestals, to film President John F. Kennedy and his entourage as they paraded in their limos through Dealey Plaza in Dallas. He had thought of not taking his camera at all but was persuaded by his staff. It proved to be a fateful choice—and for his family, a lucrative one.

He shot nearly twenty-seven seconds of film.

Eighteen of them caught the president's limousine as he was being shot, fatally. The lethal shot occurred when Zapruder, raised slightly, was nearly directly in front of the president. It is still disputed as to whether Zapruder caught the entire assassination or only the mortal part of it. By late that afternoon, a shaken Zapruder met with the Secret Service, which took the original and made two copies within three days of the assassination. He sold the original film to *Life* magazine, which ran it as selected still frames in their famous November 29, 1963, issue and then four more times over the next four years.

> The Zapruder family got the copyright to the film—Abraham died in 1970—and fought the federal government's claim of ownership based on the proposition that it was both evidence of a federal crime and significant archival material. Finally the government paid the Zapruders $16 million as part of the settlement. In the 1990s, the Zapruder heirs gave the film to the Sixth Floor Museum, housed on the very floor of the Schoolbook Depository Building (now the Dallas County Administration Building) where Lee Harvey Oswald was employed and from which he shot the president.

So what, if anything, does the film tell us about who actually shot President Kennedy? The answer is very little; after all, it only shows the victim of the shooting, not the shooter. Because Kennedy grabs at his throat and falls back, some conspiracy theorists have become convinced that a second shooter in front of the president killed him by firing from a small, sloping hill called "the grassy knoll." This is video evidence but not forensic evidence. The film is also linked to the relevant evidence supplied by Zapruder's receptionist, Marilyn Sitzman. She came along to hold her boss still on the pedestal; this was a job, given the calamitous events, for which she was eminently needed. Sitzman told the Warren Commission, which investigated the crime, that if any shots had come from the grassy knoll, where she and Zapruder themselves were standing, she would have known it.

THAT WAS THEN, THIS IS NOW: Although the Zapruder film was just one more aspect of the 1963 Kennedy trauma, it was a notable one. Without it, few Americans would have ever seen the actual, grisly horror of the assassination. With the fiftieth anniversary of the shooting, the Zapruder film was seen by eyes that had never witnessed it before. Yet it is unlikely that today's millennials will much care. Even many of their parents were not yet born when President Kennedy was murdered, so a twenty-seven-second film of the event will mean as little to them as a brief film on the Pearl Harbor attack would have meant to their parents when they were young. For Generation Y, the iconic scene of tragedy occurred on September 11, 2001, not November 22, 1963. Twenty years ago, director Oliver Stone, in *JFK*, convinced a new generation of young people that President Kennedy was killed in a vast conspiracy deep within the federal government. But what was fresh, if erroneous, conviction then has, for the current generation, turned to indifference now.

HYPOTHETICAL USAGE IN A SENTENCE BY THE OLD AND SETTLED: "Let's save this Zapruder film issue of *Life* magazine; it'll be worth something some day." —Maurice Jensen, Marshall, Texas, speaking to his family in early December 1963 (the magazine can fetch $10 today; in 1963, it cost 50 cents, or $3.87 in 2014 dollars, so Maurice's profit would be $6.13)

CONCLUSION
HERE'S YOUR CHANGE

••

n his play *The Tempest*, Shakespeare portrays a couple of villainous characters, Antonio and Ferdinand, plotting to assassinate the king of Naples while he slept. The two are out for power and wealth and have no scruples about how to attain it. Antonio says to Ferdinand, "What's past is prologue, what to come/In yours and my discharge." In other words, whatever moral hesitations might have held the two back in the past, that's merely prologue to the great thing they are about to do now. And they can do what they want; it is in *their* "discharge" (hands or power) entirely. If killing the Neapolitan monarch will make them rich, they should kill him.

Shakespeare often makes characters say something very specific, sparked by a particular situation, but then others come along and lift it into some sort of profound wisdom. Here the wisdom goes like this: "the past is prologue to the future." While this is not really what Antonio and Ferdinand mean—they mean the past is a trifle that should be forgotten about in favor of seizing their own glorious future—those who distort Shakespeare here are ironically quite right. The past really is prologue to the future—and prologue to the *present* too.

As we have seen in the foregoing pages, one can learn a lot about how we live now by comparing it with "the prologue"—how we lived then. We can learn what we think is routine and "normal" now was not always so. We can gain better insight into the present by comparing with the past, understand the new millennium better by contrasting it with how our parents and grandparents and great-grandparents lived in the twentieth century. We can learn how things have changed and how they have not. We can debate what the past tells us about the present—in doing so, we are really debating the nature of the present. We can discuss whether the apparent changes go quite deep or, alternatively, whether human nature has really not changed at all—in which case, perhaps everything fundamental has stayed the same.

Once, November 22, 1963, was the most traumatic day in American history; now, September 11, 2001 is. Once, a million dollars was a tremendous amount of money; today, some retirees with a million wonder if that's enough to get them through their nineties. Once, bound encyclopedias were a sign of middle-class aspirations and self-enhancement; now, young people have the World Wide Web. Volkswagen Beetles were once revolutionary on American roads; now, they're just another "foreign" car and are made in the USA. Plastic is now light and colorful, not heavy and monochromatic. There is no need for "liberal anticommunism" any longer. You can't put *Amos 'n' Andy* on TV.

Yet other things have not changed, such as "in character" comedy (Jack Benny and Jerry Seinfeld). Rabbit ears are making a comeback on TVs. What was once a low technology of getting a TV picture is now appealing again, ironically because of the high technology of digital streaming. Americans are still arguing about when, if ever, to become involved militarily in a foreign land. Telegrams have come back, in a way, in the form of text messages. While we are skeptical of over-the-counter tonics that promise to drive the weariness out of our blood, we still take largely untested herbals. The Goldwater revolution is still alive in the Republican Party. We still laugh, whether we do it as a result of Jack Benny or Jimmy Fallon, and cry, whether upon the death of Kennedy or the holocaust of 9/11. Even if most of our "friends" are on Facebook (where "friend" is a verb), we still value friendship. The fury and envy that prompted Arthur Godfrey to fire Julius La Rosa on the air continues to be a feature of human nature (although when Donald Trump fired people on his show, it was ostensibly because of incompetence, not too much popularity). And there is an acclaimed new HBO movie about Liberace.

So has everything changed?

Not yet.

Not quite.

The important thing is to stay tuned to the question.

BIBLIOGRAPHY

. . . .

A&P

Levinson, Marc. *The Great A&P and the Struggle for Small Business in America.* New York: Hill and Wang, 2011.

Walsh, William. *The Rise & Decline of the Great Atlantic and Pacific Tea Company.* Secaucus, NJ: Lyle Stuart Inc., 1986.

ABBOTT AND COSTELLO

Anobile, Richard J., ed. *Who's on First? Verbal and Visual Gems from the Films of Abbott & Costello.* New York: Avon Books, 1972.

Costello, Chris. *Lou's on First: The Tragic Life of Hollywood's Greatest Clown Warmly Recounted by His Youngest Child.* New York: St. Martin's Press, 1982.

"Who's on First?" Radio broadcast, 1942. http://ia600508.us.archive.org/2 /items/1940sComedy/Comedy-abbotAndCostello-WhosOnFirst 1942.mp3.

"Who's on First," with Jimmy Fallon, Jerry Seinfeld, and Billy Crystal, 2012. http://www.youtube.com/watch?v=K0Jg7pvVzKk.

AIMEE SEMPLE McPHERSON

"Aimee Semple McPherson" on *PBS American Experience*. http://www.pbs
.org/wgbh/amex/sister/.

Epstein, Daniel Mark. *Sister Aimee*. Orlando, FL: Mariner Books, 1994.

Matthew, Avery. *Aimee Semple McPherson and the Resurrection of the Christian
Experience*. Cambridge, MA: Harvard University Press, 2009.

"More Young People Are Moving Away from Religion—But Why?"
National Public Radio, January 15, 2013. http://www.npr.org/2013
/01/15/169342349/more-young-people-are-moving-away-from
-religion-but-why.

ARTHUR GODFREY

"The Man with the Barefoot Voice." *Time*, March 23, 1983.

Singer, Arthur J. *Arthur Godfrey: The Adventures of an American Broadcaster*.
Jefferson, NC: McFarland, 1999.

ARTHUR MURRAY

"Arthur Murray." *Encyclopedia of World Biography*. http://www. notable
biographies.com/supp/Supplement-Mi-So/Murray-Arthur. html.

"Arthur Murray Taught the World to Dance." *Tech Topics* (Georgia Tech
Alumni Association). Summer 1991.

Murray, Arthur. *How to Become a Good Dancer*. New York: Grove Press, 2011.

AS AMERICAN AS APPLE PIE

"As American as Apple Pie." *Cambridge Advanced Learner's Dictionary and
Thesaurus*. Cambridge: Cambridge University Press, 2011.

Avey, Tori. "What Does 'As American as Apple Pie' Really Mean?" Parade.com.
http://www.parade.com/55305/toriavey/what-does-as-american-as
-apple-pie-really-mean/.

Fierstein, Bruce. *Real Men Don't Eat Quiche*. New York: Pocket, 1982.

Millard, Ann, and Jorge Chape, *Apple Pie and Enchiladas*. Austin: University of Texas Press, 2004.

BAKELITE

"Bakelite, the Material of a Thousand Uses." Bakelite Museum. http:// www .bakelitemuseum.de.

Cook, Patrick. *Bakelite: An Illustrated Guide to Collectible Bakelite Objects*. Secaucus, NJ: Apple, 1993.

Strom, E. Thomas, and Seth Rasmussen, eds. *100+ Years of Plastic: Leo Baekeland and Beyond*. New York: Oxford University Press, 2012.

BATHTUB GIN

Blum, Deborah. "The Chemist's War." http://www.slate.com/articles/health _and_science/medical_examiner/2010/02/the_chemists_war.html.

"General Alcohol FAQs," The Alcohol and Tobacco Tax and Trade Bureau. www.ttb.gov/faqs/genalcohol.shtml.

Gublass, Alan. *Handbook of Alcoholic Beverages*. West Sussex, UK: John Wiley and Sons, 2011.

"Like Moonshine? You'll Want to Try These Six!" http://www.modernman . com/the-moonshine-brands-you-should-taste/.

Okrent, Daniel. *Last Call: The Rise and Fall of Prohibition*. New York: Scribner, 2011.

BEARDED LADY

Adams, Rachel. *Sideshow U.S.A.: Freaks and the American Cultural Imagination*. Chicago: University of Chicago Press, 2001.

Freaks. Directed by Tod Browning, 1932.

BETAMAX

Greenberg, Joshua. *From Betamax to Blockbuster*. Cambridge, MA: MIT Press, 2010.

The Virtual Museum of Vintage VCRs. http://www.totalrewind.org /mainhall.htm.

BEULAH THE BUZZER

Blumenthal, Norm. *When Game Shows Ruled Daytime TV*. Albany, GA: BearManor Media, 2010.

Truth or Consequences, 1966 episode. https://www.youtube.com/watch?v =EkD1VgtrdP8.

BILLY SUNDAY

"Billy Sunday Quotes." Brainy Quotes. http://www.brainyquote.com/quotes /authors/b/billy_sunday.html.

Bruns, Roger. *Preacher: Billy Sunday and Big-Time American Evangelism*. New York: Norton, 1992.

Carpenter, Joel A. *Revive Us Again: The Reawakening of American Fundamentalism*. New York: Oxford University Press, 1999.

"Fifty Days of Sunday." Joplin, MO, Historical Society. http://www .historicjoplin.org/?p=708.

BUCKY BEAVER

"Bucky Beaver Battles Mr. Tooth Decay." 1962 Ipana Commercial. https:// www.youtube.com/watch?v=q0po-g28uTg.

Harthill, Lane. "Whatever Happened to Ipana Toothpaste?" *Christian Science Monitor*, 1999. http://www.csmonitor.com/1999/0114/p23s3.html.

Seagrave, Kerry. *America Brushes Up: The Use and Marketing of Toothpaste in the Twentieth Century*. Jefferson, NC: McFarland, 2010.

CHARLIE CHAN

Huang, Yunte. *Charlie Chan: The Untold Story of the Honorable Detective and His Rendezvous with American History*. New York: W. W. Norton, 2011.

Mitchell, Charles P. *A Guide to Charlie Chan Films*. Westport, CT: Greenwood Press, 1999.

CHARLIE McCARTHY

Bergen, Edgar. *How to Become a Ventriloquist*. Mineola, NY: Dover, 2000.

"Charlie McCarthy." Old Time Radio. http://www.charliemccarthy.org/.

CIGARETTE GIRL

Brandt, Allan. *The Cigarette Century*. New York: Basic Books, 2009.

Cigarette Girl. Directed by John Michael McCarthy, 2009. http://www.imdb .com/title/tt1352361/.

COLLECT CALL

Fischer, Claude. *America Calling: The Social History of the Telephone until 1940*. Los Angeles: University of California Press, 1994.

"We Love You: Call Collect." http://www.snopes.com/holidays/fathersday /collect.asp.

COPYBOY

Schudson, Michael. *The News: A Social History of America's Newspapers*. New York: Basic Books, 1981.

CRIME OF THE CENTURY

Ahlgren, Gregory, and Stephen Monier. *Crime of the Century: The Lindbergh Kidnapping Hoax*. Boston: Branden Books, 2009.

Fisher, Jim. *The Lindbergh Case*. New Brunswick, NJ: Rutgers University Press, 1994.

Geis, Gilbert, and Leigh Bienen. *Crimes of the Century: From Leopold and Loeb to O. J. Simpson*. Boston: Northeastern University Press, 2000.

Scaduto, Anthony. *Scapegoat: The Lonesome Death of Bruno Richard Hauptmann*. New York: Putnam, 1976.

DEWEY DEFEATS TRUMAN

Mallon, Thomas. *Dewey Defeats Truman*. New York: Pantheon Books, 1997.

Pietrusza, David. *1948: Truman's Improbable Victory*. New York: Union Square Press, 2011.

DING DONG SCHOOL

Berger, Daniel, and Steve Jajkowski, eds. *Chicago Television: Images of America*. Chicago: Arcadia, 2010.

Horwich, Frances, and Reinald Werrenrath Jr. *The Robin Family: A Ding Dong School Book*. Skokie, IL: Rand McNally, 1954.

DON AMECHE

Ohmart, Ben. *Don Ameche: The Kenosha Comeback Kid*. Albany, GA: BearManor Media, 2007.

DO NOT FOLD, BEND, SPINDLE, OR MUTILATE

Bashe, Charles J., et al. *IBM's Early Computers*. Cambridge, MA: MIT Press, 1986.

Yost, Jeffrey. *The IBM Century*. Piscataway, NJ: IEEE Computer Society Press, 2011.

DUM-DEE-DUM-DUM

"The Big Crime," *Dragnet* episode, September 9, 1954. https://archive.org
/details/Dragnet_TheBigCrime.

Webb, Jack. *The Badge: True and Terrifying Stories That Could Not Be Presented on TV*. New York: Da Capo Press, 2005.

EDSEL

Deutsch, Jan. *The Edsel and Corporate Responsibility*. New Haven, CT: Yale University Press, 1976.

"Henry Ford" on *PBS American Experience*. http://www.pbs.org/wgbh/americanexperience/films/henryford/.

"EFFETE CORPS OF IMPUDENT SNOBS"

Perlstein, Rick. *Nixonland*. New York: Scribner, 2008.

EIGHT-TRACK

So Wrong They're Right. Directed by Russ Forster, 1995.

"Vintage Audio History." http://www.videointerchange.com/audio_history.htm.

EMILY POST

Elias, Norbert. *The History of Manners*. Vol. 1. New York: Pantheon, 1982.

Post, Emily. *Emily Post's Etiquette*. New York: Empire Books, 2013.

EXTREMISM IN THE DEFENSE OF LIBERTY

Perlstein, Rick. *Before the Storm: Barry Goldwater and the Unmaking of the American Consensus*. New York: Nation Books, 2009.

FATTY ARBUCKLE

Oderman, Stuart. *Roscoe "Fatty" Arbuckle*. Jefferson, NC: McFarland, 2005.

FLUB-A-DUB

Davis, Stephen. *Say, Kids! What Time Is It?* New York: Little, Brown, 1987.

Miller, Douglas, and Marion Nowak. *The Fifties: The Way We Really Were.* New York: VNR AG, 1977.

FORTY-FIVE (45) RPM

Dawson, Jim, and Steve Propes. *45 RPM.* San Francisco: Backbeat Books, 2003.

Millard, Andre. *America on Record: A History of Recorded Sound.* Cambridge: Cambridge University Press, 2005.

FRANCIS THE TALKING MULE

Bartel, Pauline. *Amazing Animal Actors.* New York: Taylor Publishing, 1997.

Stern, David. *Francis the Talking Mule.* New York: Farrar, Strauss, and Co., 1946.

GEORGE "KINGFISH" STEVENS

Amos 'n' Andy. Radio show archive. https://archive.org/details/amosandy1.

Amos 'n' Andy. TV show archive. http://www.tv.com/shows/amos-n-andy/.

Ely, Melvin Patrick. *The Adventures of Amos 'n' Andy.* Charlottesville: University of Virginia Press, 2001.

GOING GARBO

The Divine Garbo. Directed by Bjorn Hessie, 2010. https://www.youtube.com/watch?v=vvv686mnPV8.

Swenson, Karen. *Greta Garbo: A Life Apart.* New York: Scribner, 1997.

GOOD EVENING, MR. AND MRS. AMERICA, AND ALL THE SHIPS AT SEA

Gabler, Neil. *Winchell: Gossip, Power, and the Culture of Celebrity.* New York: Vintage, 1994.

HOPALONG CASSIDY

Boyd, Grace, and Michael Cochran. *Hopalong Cassidy: An American Legend*. York, PA: Gemstone, 2008.

"Hoppy Days." http://hopalongcassidyfestival.com.

Miller, Lee O., and Joel McCrea. *The Great Cowboy Stars of Movies and Television*. New York: Arlington House, 1979.

IN LIKE FLYNN

Flynn, Errol, and Jeffery Meyers. *My Wicked, Wicked Ways*. New York: Cooper Square Press, 2002.

"Swashbuckler." *Oxford Dictionary.* http://blog.oxforddictionaries. com/2012/05 /origin-of-swashbuckler/.

ISOLATION BOOTH

Long, Susan. "The 1958 Quiz Show Scandal." http://j210quizshowscandal susanlong.blogspot.com/.

Quiz Show. Directed by Robert Redford, 1994.

Stone, Joseph, and Tim Yohn. *Prime Time and Misdemeanors: Investigating the 1950s TV Quiz Sandal—A D.A.'s Account*. New Brunswick, NJ: Rutgers University Press, 1994.

JOHN BERESFORD TIPTON

The Millionaire. Plot summaries of episodes, 1955–1960. http://www.imdb .com/title/tt0047758/.

JUNGLE JIM

Fury, David. *Johnny Weissmuller: Twice the Hero*. Minneapolis, MN: Thorndike Press, 2001.

Jungle Jim. Plot summaries of episodes, 1955–1956. http://www.imdb.com /title/tt0047747/episodes?year=1955&ref_=tt_eps_yr_1955.

KING OF THE WILD FRONTIER

Chemerka, William, Phil Collins, and Ron Ely. *Fess Parker: TV's Frontier Hero.* Albany, GA: BearManor Media, 2011.

"Davy Crockett: Indian Fighter." Miniseries episode, 1954. https://www .youtube.com/watch?v=HtjUt1MtFlY.

"LET IT ALL HANG OUT"

Farber, David. *The Age of Great Dreams: America in the 1960s.* New York: Hill and Wang, 1994.

The Hombres. "Let It All Hang Out." https://www.youtube.com /watch?v=XWN65nAkk20.

LIBERACE

Byron, Darden Asbury. *Liberace: An All-American Boy.* Chicago: University of Chicago Press, 2000.

LIBERAL ANTICOMMUNISM

Halberstam, David. *The Fifties.* New York: Ballantine Books, 1994.

Wald, Alan. *New York Intellectuals: The Rise and Decline of the Anti-Stalinist Left from the 1930s to the 1980s.* Chapel Hill, NC: University of North Carolina Press, 1987.

LISTEN TO THE WARM

"Allen Ginsberg." *PBS American Masters.* http://www.pbs.org/wnet /americanmasters/database/ginsberg_a.html.

McKuen, Rod. *Listen to the Warm.* New York: Random House, 1967.

McKuen, Rod. *Stanyon Street and Other Sorrows*. New York: Random House, 1970.

Meyer, David S. *The Politics of Protest: Social Movements in America*. New York: Oxford University Press, 2007.

THE LONG BRANCH

Barabas, SuzAnn, and Gabor Barabas. *Gunsmoke: The Complete History and Analysis*. Jefferson, NC: McFarland, 1990.

"The Noose." *Gunsmoke* TV episode, 1970 https://www.youtube.com /watch?v=_U3eK35h0_Q.

"Shakespeare." *Gunsmoke* radio episode, 1952. https://archive.org/details / OTRR_Gunsmoke_Singles.

LSMFT

Brandt, Alan. *The Cigarette Century*. New York: Basic Books, 2009.

Gladwell, Malcolm. *The Tipping Point*. New York: Back Bay Books, 2002.

"Lucky Strike cigarette commercial," 1948. https://www.youtube.com /watch?v=ZQ8znH0wSiU.

MADE IN JAPAN

Dower, John. *Embracing Defeat: Japan in the Wake of World War II*. New York: W. W. Norton, 1999.

White, Carole B. *Collector's Encyclopedia of Made in Japan Ceramics*. Paducah, KY: Collector Books, 2005.

"Why Is It Marked Occupied Japan?" http://www.ebay.com/gds/Why-is-it -marked-Occupied-Japan-/10000000002442354/g.html.

"World's Richest Countries." http://www.worldsrichestcountries.com/top _japan_exports.html.

MILTOWN

Junig, J. T. "Europe Dumps Meprobamate." http://www.suboxonetalkzone
.com/europe-dumps-meprobamate/.

Tone, Andrea. *The Age of Anxiety: A History of America's Turbulent Affair with
Tranquilizers.* New York: Basic Books, 2009.

"Tranquilizer Put Under U.S. Curbs: Side-Effects Noted." *New York Times*
reprint of UPI story, December 6, 1967. http://select.nytimes
.com/gst/abstract.html?res=F6081FFD3A5B1A7B93C4A917
89D95F438685F9.

MIMEOGRAPH

Hutchison, Howard. *Mimeograph: Operation Maintenance and Repair.* Blue
Ridge Summit, PA: Tab Books, 1979.

Owen, David. *Copies in Seconds.* New York: Simon and Schuster, 2004.

THE ORIGINAL AMATEUR HOUR

"Major Bowes Dies at Home in New Jersey." *Pittsburgh Post-Gazette,* June
14, 1946.

The Original Amateur Hour. Hosted by Pat Boone, 2 DVD set.

PERCY DOVETONSILS

"Leslie the Animal Trainer." Recited by Ernie Kovacs playing Percy Dovetonsils.
https://www.youtube.com/watch?v=he3s9gQ134Y.

Rico, Diana. *Kovacsland.* Orlando, FL: Harcourt, Brace and Jovanovich, 1990.

QUEEN FOR A DAY

Cassidy, Marsha. *What Women Watched: Daytime Television in the 1950s.*
Austin: University of Texas Press, 2005.

Queen for a Day. March 1958 episode. https://www.youtube.com/watch?v
=MwunZq8H1s0.

RABBIT EARS

Mullen, Megan. *The Rise of Cable Programming in the United States.* Austin:
University of Texas Press, 2003.

"REALLY BIG SHEW"

Leonard, John. "The Ed Sullivan Age." *American Heritage Magazine*, Vol. 48,
no. 3 (May/June 1997).

Maguire, James. *Impresario: The Life and Times of Ed Sullivan.* New York:
Billboard Books, 2011.

RECORD HOP

Sagolia, Lisa Jo. *Rock 'n' Roll Dances of the 1950s.* Westport, CT: Greenwood
Press, 2011.

Singer, Artie, John Medora, and David White. "At the Hop." Performed
by Danny and the Juniors. https://www.youtube.com/watch?v
=HlXMKA7d4to.

ROAD PICTURES

Lamour, Dorothy, and Dick McInnes. *My Side of the Road.* Englewood Cliffs,
NJ: Prentice Hall, 1980.

"The 'Road' of Hope, Crosby, and Lamour." http://h2g2.com/approved_entry
/A2622809.

RUNNING BOARD

Car: The Definitive Visual history of the Automobile. New York: DK Adult, 2011.

Helmer, William J., and Rick Mattix. *The Complete Public Enemies Almanac.* Nashville, TN: Cumberland House, 2007.

Vallée, Rudy, and the Yale Men. "Doin' the Raccoon." https://www.youtube .com/watch?v=lg3-ZcGcsms.

SHE WEARS THE PANTS IN THE FAMILY

Flexner, Eleanor. *Century of Struggle: The Women's Rights Movement in the United States.* Cambridge, MA: Belknap Press, 1996.

Smith, Catherine, and Cynthia Greig. *Women Wearing Pants.* New York: Harry N. Abrams, 2003.

SINGING TELEGRAM

"Classic Sesame Street: Grover Delivers A Singing Telegram." https://www .youtube.com/watch?v=VnGzpoDK_xQ.

Coe, Lewis. *Telegraph.* Jefferson, NC: McFarland, 2003.

"Heart." *Glee* episode wiki, February 14, 2012. http://glee.wikia.com/wiki/Heart.

SLIDE RULE

Hopp, Peter. *Slide Rules.* Apple Valley, MN: Astragal Press, 1999.

"'TAIN'T FUNNY, MCGEE"

Fibber McGee and Molly. Radio show archive. https://archive.org/details /FibberMcGeeandMolly1940.

Schulz, Clair. *Fibber McGee and Molly, On the Air.* Albany, GA: BearManor Media, 2008.

TELEPHONE NOOK

Meyer, Ralph O. *Old-Time Telephones! Design, History, and Restoration.* Atglen, PA: Schiffer Publications, Ltd., 2005.

New, Catherine. "Smartphones Are Used by Nearly Half of Americans." http://www.huffingtonpost.com/2012/03/01/most-americans-have -a-smartphone_n_1314914.html.

Rybczynski, Witold. *Home: A Short History of an Idea.* New York: Penguin, 1987.

"Telecommunication Timeline." http://www.schoelles.com/Telephone /teltimeline.htm.

T FORMATION

Bible, Dana. *Championship Football.* Upper Saddle Hill, NJ: Prentice-Hall, 1947.

MacCambridge, Michael. *America's Game.* New York: Anchor, 2005.

TIRED BLOOD

Didion, Joan. *Blue Nights.* New York: Vintage, 2011.

"Geritol's Bitter Pill." *Time,* February 5, 1973. http://content.time.com/time /magazine/article/0,9171,906840,00.html.

Rapp, Robert. *The Pill Book Guide to Over-the-Counter Medications.* New York: Bantam, 1997.

"UM, THAT RIGHT, KEMOSABE"

"Enter the Lone Ranger." *Lone Ranger* episode, 1949. https://www.youtube .com/watch?v=V71lU68QZzg.

Pew Research. "Religious Landscape Survey." http://religions.pewforum.org /reports.

Striker, Fran. *The Lone Ranger Rides.* New York: KHE Global, 2003.

Van Hise, James. *Who Was That Masked Man?* Pioneer Books, 1990.

VOLKSWAGEN JOKES

Rieger, Bernhard. *The People's Car*. Cambridge, MA: Harvard University Press, 2013.

WATERGATE

Emery, Fred. *Watergate*. New York: Touchstone, 1995.

The Final Report: Watergate. Documentary by National Geographic Channel. https://www.youtube.com/watch?v=nFID6Qkwh88.

"WE HAD TO DESTROY THE VILLAGE IN ORDER TO SAVE IT"

Caputo, Philip. *A Rumor of War*. New York: Holt, 1996.

Keyes, Ralph. *The Quote Verifier: Who Said What, Where, and When*. New York: St. Martin's Griffin, 2006.

The Vietnam War, 1964–76. Documentary. https://www.youtube.com/watch?v=yj1X2WpiiOE.

WORLD BOOK

Brown, Andrew. *A Brief History of Encyclopedias*. London: Hesperus Press, 2011.

World Book. http://store.worldbook.com/?.

YOUR HIT PARADE

Cox, Jim. *Music Radio: The Great Performers and Programs of the 1920s through Early 1960s*. Jefferson, NC: McFarland, 2005.

"Heartbreak Hotel." Performed by Snooky Lanson, 1956. https://www.youtube.com/watch?v=Kb81NDtbZpI.

Your Hit Parade. Episode from February 27, 1954. https://www.youtube.com/watch?v=J0iTZdpHfeA.

YOUR MONEY OR YOUR LIFE

Benny, Jack, and Joan Benny. *Sunday Nights at Seven*. New York: Warner Books, 1990.

"Your Money or Your Life." Original radio feature, 1948. https://www .youtube.com/watch?v=-tVzdUczMT0.

THE ZAPRUDER FILM

Bugliosi, Vincent. *Reclaiming History: The Assassination of President John F. Kennedy*. New York: W. W. Norton, 2007.

Posner, Gerald. *Case Closed*. New York: Anchor, 2003.

"Zapruder Film, Frame by Frame." https://www.youtube.com/watch?v =A1Lyv4wrJQU.

INDEX

B

C

ACKNOWLEDGMENTS

We thank our agent, Steve Harris, whose loyalty to this project and his success in presenting it, were exemplary.

Thanks to our superb and exacting editors at Sourcebooks, Stephanie Bowen and Jenna Skwarek.

We appreciate our significant others, Joanna and Sarah, for putting up with our incessant chatter about the project over the past months.

Finally, we must thank our parents, who worked hard to give us access, when we were kids, to the mid-century cultural agendas that populate this book.

ABOUT THE AUTHORS

Tom McBride, emeritus English professor of Beloit College, where he taught Shakespeare for forty-one years, has published many essays on a wide variety of subjects, including Saul Bellow, Sherlock Holmes, Raymond Carver, and Ludwig Wittgenstein. A former commentator on Wisconsin Public Radio and director of Beloit's First Year Initiative Program, he is coauthor with Ron Nief of the annual Beloit College Mindset List and *The Mindset Lists of American History* (John Wiley and Sons, 2011). He and Nief are frequent speakers around the country.

Ron Nief is emeritus director of public affairs at Beloit College in Wisconsin, having stepped down in 2009 after fourteen years at the liberal arts college. A *Mad Men*–era veteran of Madison Avenue, his work at Beloit concludes four decades communicating the work of higher education starting with his alma mater, Boston College, and continuing at such schools as Brandeis and Middlebury. He is the editor of several books and has written for the *New York Times*, the *Boston Globe*, the *Christian Science Monitor*, Gannett Newspapers, and National Public Radio. He created the Mindset List in 1998 and joins Tom McBride in many media appearances and talks around the country throughout the year.